HOW TO COLLECT STAMPS

ANOTHER FINE PRODUCT FROM

H.E. Harris & Co., Inc.®

BOSTON, MASS. 02117

The World's Largest Stamp Firm—Founded in 1916

INTERNATIONAL STANDARD BOOK NUMBER (ISBN): 0-937458-00-7

Fellow Collector,

Over the years, literally thousands of stamp collectors like yourself have turned to Harris and asked us, as leaders in the stamp industry, to create a stamp collector's handbook designed *specifically for practical everyday use,* one that would answer the most frequently-asked questions and provide the most frequently-sought information.

The Harris *How to Collect Stamps* is just such a book, and more: comprehensive, yet eminently readable, it is no story book or history book to be read through once, then put away on a shelf; rather, it is a true reference work, one that you will want to keep close at hand at all times.

No matter what your age or level of collecting experience — beginner or advanced — you will find this book to be an indispensable aid in deriving the maximum possible enjoyment from stamp collecting. Along with your album and catalogue, it is *the* book which you will be using most consistently and profitably.

The fully illustrated World-Wide and U.S. Stamp Identifiers are the largest and most comprehensive to be found in any book of this kind; the illustrated Collector's Dictionary explains, clearly and concisely, most of the common philatelic terms collectors are likely to encounter; and the exclusive 19-page map section includes not only present-day stamp-issuing countries, but all the vanished lands as well, countries which once issued stamps, but no longer exist.

Practical tables give Arabic equivalents of foreign numerals, and high-quality paper, sturdy covers, and a special binding ensure that this volume will withstand the most constant daily use.

The Harris *How to Collect Stamps* is the result of years of meticulous research and close attention to collector's desires, combined with Harris' unparalleled expertise; it is sure to become one of your most valuable and highly-prized stamp collecting accessories.

Yours truly,
H. E. HARRIS & CO., INC.

Wesley Mann

Wesley P. Mann, Jr.
President

COLLECTING IS THE OLDEST HOBBY!

Man is a born collector — since time immemorial, he has been collecting all sorts of things, for all sorts of different reasons. The first collector was probably a caveman who found some unusually attractive rocks and decided to take them home. Or it may **have** been some bones to which he attached some supernatural significance, or some shells, or feathers — no matter. What is important is that today, more people are collectors than any other type of hobbyist; and more people by far collect stamps than any other object.

Why stamps? Think of all the different things that people collect — antiques, magazines, bottles, coins, rocks, automobiles, works of art, even autographs — and the reasons why they collect them — aesthetic appeal, cultural or historical significance, curiosity, nostalgia value, pride of ownership, or just plain whimsy — and you'll find that stamp collecting offers all these attractions combined, and more!

Aesthetic appeal? You would need a museum larger than the fabulous Louvre to house all the marvelous paintings, magnificent statues, and other great works of art to be found on stamps. The Mona Lisa, Venus de Milo, Rodin's "The Thinker," Rembrandts, Michelangelos, Picassos, Van Goghs — they're all here. And many collectors consider stamps themselves, with their finely-executed designs and exquisite details, to be miniature works of art in their own right.

Cultural and historical significance? Through stamps you'll gain knowledge about the manners, customs, dress, traditions, and folklore of people in all parts of the globe. You'll witness events which shaped the world as it is today, meet heroic figures of the past, and catch futuristic glimpses of things to come.

Curiosity? Nothing will whet your curiosity like the hundreds of strange and unknown people, events, and other subjects you'll find on stamps, You'll delve through history, geography, science, sports, every **subject** known to man seeking the answers to questions posed by your stamps.

Nostalgia? Antique autos, people dressed as they were years ago, old buildings long since torn down, figures from the past — they're all on stamps. Pride of ownership? Just watch a stamp collector beam as he regards a new acquisition, or straightens out the volumes in his collection. Whimsy? There are stamps picturing scenes from fairy tales, cartoon characters, imaginary space creatures, and more.

And stamp collecting has other virtues, too. It offers relaxation, rejuvenation of the spirit, an escape from the cares of the everyday world. It offers the excitement of the hunt, the unknown, as you pore through a pile of stamps hoping to find something of value, perhaps even a great rarity!

Through stamp collecting, too, you can make new friends, and strengthen existing relationships. One of the pleasures of stamp collecting is meeting with other collectors, to swap stamps, discuss finer philatelic points, and in general share your interest in the hobby. Families find that stamp collecting offers an excellent way to spend time together; and stamp collectors find they have much in common with other collectors in their neighborhood, city, state, other states, even other countries. Stamp collecting provides a common ground for understanding between peoples, near and far. As stamp collector Lily Pons, the famed opera star, said, "Stamp collecting — like music — makes one part of a great world-wide fraternity knowing no bounds of nationality."

It is no wonder, then, that famous people from every walk of life — presidents, kings and queens, businessmen, movie stars, religious leaders, musicians, military leaders — have all been avid stamp collectors.

As President Franklin D. Roosevelt said, "Stamp collecting dispels boredom, enlarges our visions, broadens our knowledge, makes for better citizens, and in innumerable ways enriches our life."

A BRIEF HISTORY OF STAMP COLLECTING

Who was the first stamp collector? No one knows for sure, but it can't have been too long after the first stamps were issued that someone thought it would be a grand idea to collect these little bits of postal paper, as novelties or souvenirs. As more and more countries adopted the new postal system, and the number of different stamps from different countries began to grow, other people took interest, and the hobby of philately was under way.

Of course, it was easier to collect stamps then. There were no decisions that had to be made over what countries or topics to collect — nearly everyone was a worldwide collector. Ten years after the introduction of the Penny Black, only 153 more stamps had been introduced; in 1860, the total number of stamps was still under 1,000. But the number of stamps and stamp-issuing countries and colonies increased rapidly thereafter, and today there are well over 200,000 different stamps — not including all the minor varieties, errors, reprints, and so forth.

Then, as today, people gathered stamps for many different reasons: one woman advertised for used Penny Blacks to paper her walls; another wanted to use the stamps to decorate her lampshades. The first known advertisement for stamps for actual hobby-collecting purposes appeared in the London *Family Herald* in 1851. It was probably through such advertisements that stamp collectors first made contact with each other, and formed the first stamp clubs and philatelic societies. The very first philatelic society on record was called the Omnibus Club, and was formed in the

4

United States in 1856. Today, there are many different philatelic societies in many countries, and an international society called FIP — the Federation Internationale de Philatelie, founded in 1926.

As for the use of the word "philately" to describe stamp collecting, it first appears in an article written in 1864 by a French stamp collector named Herpin for a French stamp magazine. Derived from two Greek roots, "philo," meaning "love," and "atelos," meaning something exempt from "taxes," i.e., a letter with postage paid, the word was used to mean "love of postage stamps." The term gained such widespread popularity — many people must have thought it described exactly the way they felt-that it was incorporated into common usage.

Some people in those early days of philately may have thought that stamp collecting was just a passing fancy, a short-lived fad — time has proven them very wrong. Interest in stamp collecting has grown steadily through the years until today countless people throughout the world — and more than 16 million in the United States alone — turn to stamp collecting for both recreation and pleasure, making it truly "The World's Most Popular Hobby."

* * * * * * * *

A BRIEF HISTORY OF POSTAGE STAMPS.

The first organized system for carrying written messages was established by the Persians under Darius, who created a network of mounted couriers stationed at various points throughout his vast empire, ready to speed letters to any part of the country. These early "Pony Express" riders were so efficient that they inspired the ancient Greek historian Herodotus to coin the famous phrase which appears on the facade of the New York City post office building: "Neither snow nor rain nor heat nor gloom of night stays these couriers form the swift completion of their appointed rounds.

Darius' system was adopted and expanded upon by Caesar Augustus, whose "Cursus Publicus" included couriers on foot, on horseback, and in carriages, travelling well-maintained highways connecting Rome with every outlying territory of the Roman Empire. The "Cursus Publicus" was known familiarly as the "post" system because of the way-stations, or posts, established at regular intervals along each route to provide the couriers with food and fresh horses.

The first postal system open to the public (the earlier ones had all been exclusively for royal use) was established in 1505 by the Thurn and Taxis families of Austria, who offered to carry letters and parcels anywhere in continental Europe for anyone who could pay the fee. Organized under a royal license, the Thurn and Taxis system survived for more than 350 years, well into the modern postal era.

The Thurn and Taxis system was privately-owned, and so was the London Penny Post when it was inaugurated in 1680 by a businessman named William Dockwra. But the Penny Post proved to be so profitable that the government, seeing in it an ideal source of internal revenue, decided to take over its operation for itself. Thus was born, in 1698, the first public postal system.

Dockwra's Penny Post was a model of Postal efficiency, and it remains so even to this day. Letter-boxes were posted at hundreds of points throughout London, and branch offices were established in every district. For one penny, a letter or parcel deposited at a letter box or branch station would be picked up, handstamped to indicate the time of collection and certify that the postage had been paid, and delivered to any address in the city. Deliveries were made every hour in the business district and from four to eight times a day in the outlying sections.

In colonial America, meanwhile, the first post office had been established at Boston in 1639, and by 1691 a uniform postal service was in operation throughout the colonies. The first postal system of the new government of the United States went into operation in 1775, with Benjamin Franklin as the first Postmaster General.

Until 1840, however, all these systems operated without the benefit of a postage stamp. Items were handstamped mostly to show receipt at a post office, and postage was collected from the addressee upon delivery. Many people developed secret codes by which they could cheat the postal services: secret marks on the outside of the envelope conveyed the sender's message, and all the addressee had to do was to read the secret message on the envelope, then refuse to accept the letter and pay the fee.

To counter this trend, Sir Rowland Hill, the British Postmaster General, created the first adhesive postage stamp in 1840 — and the modern postal era was born. The stamps were to be bought beforehand by the person wishing to send a letter, then affixed to the letter, indicating that the postage had been paid. The stamps were designed by Hill himself, and bore a profile likeness of the young Queen Victoria, who had just come to the throne three years before. Because they were printed in black, the one-cent stamps became known as "Penny Blacks" — and were the first government-printed postage stamps.

This new postal system of collecting the postage in advance proved immensely popular, and it was not long before all the civilized countries in the world had instituted like systems. The United States itself issued its first stamps in 1847, a 5¢ Franklin and a 10¢ Washington.

As more and more nations joined the postal fraternity, the frontiers between them began to cause numerous difficulties. Different nations had different postal rates, transportation fees, and internal conditions, so the delivery of mail over international boundaries involved the negotiation of complicated and confusing bilateral written treaties. Mail from Spain to Germany, for example, had to travel from Spain to France under one treaty, and from France to Germany under another — and might be stopped altogether if the treaty expired while the mail was en route. An obvious need existed for a broad international postal system to replace the multitude of bilateral treaties.

One of the early leaders in the movement for an international postal organization was Montgomery Blair, the U.S. Postmaster Gerneral. It was mostly through Blair's efforts that the first international postal conference was convened in Paris in 1863, attended by the United States and 15 European Nations. Though an international postal organization was not founded in Paris, many of the proposals forwarded at the conference, such as standardization of postal weights and rates, influenced the agreement which finally emerged 12 years later.

In the following years, the initiative in the international movement was taken over by the German Postmaster General, Dr. Heinrich von Stephan, who worked hard to draft proposals which would make the flow of mail between countries as simple and efficient as the flow of mail within countries. His years of labor bore fruit in October, 1874, when 22 countries met in the first Postal Congress in Berne, Switzerland, and founded the Universal Postal Union. The final agreement, which took place in July, 1875, included such principles as a unified rate for letters, the principle that the postage is paid by the sender, standardized delivery and transportation fees, etc.

Today, all civilized nations of the world belong to the U.P.U. In addition to expediting the world-wide distribution of mail, the U.P.U. also regulates international disputes and problems which may arise from time to time. It has been said that of all international organizations, the U.P.U. is the one body which comes closest to successfully fulfilling its original goals.

FAMOUS RARITIES

Mention stamp collecting to the average non-collector, and chances are the first thing that will come to his mind will be some story he has heard in the past about a rare stamp being sold for a fabulous amount of money. And in truth, such tales are as much a part of the hobby as are the stamps themselves.

For example, practically every collector (and many non-collectors as well) knows the story of the 1856 British Guiana one cent magenta, the world's rarest stamp. Found in an attic by an English schoolboy in 1873, and sold to a friend for $1.50, this one stamp was valued in 1980 at $850,000.

Other famous rarities include the 1847 Mauritus 1¢ and 2¢ issues accidentally printed "Post Office" instead of "Post Paid," and worth $250,000 a piece (all values given here are 1980 Standard Catalog prices); the 1851 2¢ Hawaiian Missionary stamp, valued at $110,000, Spain's 1851 2 reale stamp, printed in blue instead of red and worth $135,000, and another color error, the 1851 Baden 9 kreuzer green (it should have been red), valued at $60,000.

Famous United States rarities include most of the 1846-47 Postmaster's Provisionals, particularly the Alexandria, Va. 5¢ "Blue Boy" worth $85,000, the Boscawen, N.H. 5¢, and the Lockport, N.Y. 5¢, valued at $85,000.00 apiece; the 1869 Landing of Columbus" 15¢ stamp with inverted center, worth $80,000, the 1869 "Shield, Eagle, and Flags" 30¢ stamp with inverted Flags, worth $50,000; and the most famous U.S. rarity of all, the 1918 "Curtiss Jenny" 24¢ airmail with inverted center, valued at $100,000.

What makes these little pieces of paper worth so much money? The answer lies in the age-old law of supply and demand: in the more than 100 years since the 1856 British Guiana was discovered, no other copy has come to light. Meanwhile the number of collectors in the world has grown into the tens of millions, all of whom would like to own this one stamp. It's no wonder, then, that the price has risen to such astonishing heights!

Of course, the chances of finding any of the really old rare stamps grow slimmer each day, with so many millions of collectors engaged in the search; but important philatelic finds are still being made, usually as they have always been made in the past: by someone browsing through a collection of old letters, cleaning out an attic, thumbing through a pile of old documents, etc.

The best place to look for valuable stamps is anywhere mail has been saved or accumulated for many years. Attics, basements, storage rooms, etc., often yield old trunks or bundles containing letters from grandparents or even great-grandparents. Among these letters there is always the possibility that a valuable stamp will be found.

Many businesses, banks and other financial concerns, schools, county courthouses, churches, etc., store their correspondence and records for years; some of the greatest stamp finds have been made among such ancient papers.

A stamp does not necessarily have to be very old, however, to be extremely valuable — the law of supply and demand applies to modern stamps as well as to ancient ones.

In 1954, for example, a copy of the newly-minted Kenya 5c stamp picturing the Owen Falls Dam was found to have a picture of the dam inverted. Millions of "correct" copies of this stamp were printed, and at least 400 copies of the error have existed at one time, since the stamps were printed in 100-stamp sheets, four sheets to a pane. But no other copy of the stamp with the "upside-down dam" has ever turned up, the one-of-a-kind stamp was eventually purchased by a wealthy Indian maharajah for a price estimated to be around $10,000, and its value today is considered to be many times that sum.

CORRECTLY PRINTED   ERROR

Again, as recently as 1962, a sheet of Canal Zone "Thatcher Ferry Bridge" 4¢ stamps was found which had the picture of the bridge erroneously omitted. Eighteen years later, these stamps were valued at $5,500.00 a piece.

This last case, incidentally, was one of great importance to all collectors. The Thatcher Ferry Bridge find was made by H.E. Harris, founder of the famous stamp firm which bears his name, and one of the great pioneers of the stamp hobby. When the Canal Zone postal authorities learned of Harris' discovery, they proposed to print millions of additional stamps with the bridge omitted—deliberate "errors" which would have rendered Harris' copies worthless as rarities.

Harris went to court to protect his find, and in a landmark decision, the postal authorities were enjoined from any action which would devalue the genuine errors. This decision set a legal precedent which assures every collector who even dreams of finding a valuable error that any such discovery cannot be rendered worthless through deliberate government interference.

This hope of someday discovering a rare stamp, no matter how remote the chances may be, adds much to the excitement of stamp collecting — but it is still only a small part of the larger pleasures the hobby has to offer. What makes a stamp valuable is the fact that, though millions of people may want one, only a very select few collectors will ever be privileged to own a copy of it, thus, a collector whose only interest in the hobby lies in the acquisition of great rarities is almost certain to be disappointed.

Obviously, then, the millions of people in the world today who collect stamps must do so for some reason other than the simple acquisition of rarities. And, although much has been said time and again about the many virtues of the hobby — it is educational, it brings people together, it is relaxing, it teaches good habits, etc.— the one overriding fact that remains is this: stamp collecting is fun!

WHERE AND HOW TO GET STAMPS

So you've decided to become a stamp collector, and have even bought an album — now, how and where can you acquire stamps? For a starter, you can look for old letters and documents stored away in your own attic or basement; you can ask a friend who works in a bank or church to save stamps for you from incoming foreign mail; and you can save stamps from your own correspondence with friends, relatives and business acquaintances.

But these traditional sources of supply will soon become inadequate; then, you will find that your two principal methods of acquiring stamps are to: 1) purchase them; and 2) get them from other collectors by swapping your own duplicates.

Many beginning collectors will be attracted by the accumulations, or mixtures, often found at stamp dealers and retail stores under such names as "Big Bag of Stamps," "Bonus Bag of Stamps," or "Golden Galleon Mixture." Such mixtures usually contain a specified number or volume of stamps, unpicked and unsorted, many still on the original bits of paper on which they were used.

Though these mixtures offer a huge number of stamps for the money, one should bear in mind that the condition will not always be the best, that there are usually many duplicates, and that the stamps will normally be of the very commonest variety. Nonetheless, you will often find some very desirable issues in a mixture, and precisely because the stamps are unpicked and unsorted, it is not unknown for a really valuable item to appear in one of these accumulations. At the very least, a mixture is sure to give you your money's worth in stamps, plus hours of fun.

The best bet for a beginning collector, however, is a packet of all different stamps. These packets offer the stamps already off paper and in better condition than one would find in a mixture, and come in three general catagories; world-wide; from a specific country, continent, or group of countries; and of a specific type or topic, such as airmails or flowers. Packets are available with as few as 5 or 10 stamps, or as many as several thousand varieties.

A good rule of thumb when buying a packet is to get the largest one you can possibly afford, and buy a world-wide packet first. Then, you can supplement this first group of stamps with packets of stamps from individual countries, until you have a nice, well-rounded collection, at the same time keeping duplication to a minimum.

The next step after packets is to buy stamps in sets. Packets will rarely contain complete sets of stamps, so you will usually find yourself with one or two stamps each from many different sets. The most economical way to complete these broken sets is to buy a complete set from a dealer (or if you are very lucky, you may find a short set which is missing precisely the values you already have), keep the values you need, and swap the duplicates.

Even then, you will still have blank spaces in your album; either you were unable to get particular stamps in any of the preveious methods, or you have some sets which are just missing one or two values and it would not be economical to buy a complete set just to fill those few spaces. Then you must look for the individual stamps. This is, of course, a more expensive level of stamp collecting.

When you are shopping for single specimens, the first place to look is, of course, a stamp dealer; you can either look through his stock books or stamps he may have on display, or you may prepare a "want list" of the items you are seeking. Such a list would include the country, catalog number, and condition of the stamp. If you are submitting your want list through the mail, you might also want to include the price you are willing to pay for each item. Upon receipt of your want list, the dealer will then locate the individual items, price them, and submit them for your examination.

As a last resort, if you cannot locate an item at a dealer's, you can advertise in a newspaper or stamp magazine, club newsletter or bulletin board, or even by word of mouth, for the stamp you want. With any luck, there's certain to be a collector somewhere who will have a duplicate copy of exactly the item you are looking for.

One of the most enjoyable ways to shop for stamps, especially for the beginner, is "on approval." At your request, a dealer will send you packets, sheets, or booklets of stamps at regular intervals for you to examine in the comfort of your own home. You select the items you want and return the balance, usually within ten days at the most, along with your payment for the stamps you have kept; the service can be cancelled at any time you desire.

Most mail order firms which offer stamps on approval have prepared stamp packets which are specially selected to cater to the individual collector's level of interest. A beginner's approval selection would include a wide variety of subjects and countries to broaden the novice's interest in and knowledge of stamps; an intermediate selection would be narrower in scope, as the collector would have indicated either through his previous purchases or through correspondence, the direction his preferences were taking; and a selection sent to an advanced collector would be narrower still. Throughout the world, there are many such stamp firms who have "Approval" services, taking great pains to ensure that every selection sent to each approval customer is specifically designed to help build that individual's collection to the highest possible level.

Other places where collectors can purchase stamps include auctions, where bids can usually be placed either in person or by mail; stamp club sales books, which usually contain club members' duplicates; direct from government post offices or philatelic agencies, especially where new issues are concerned; and from advertisements in stamp magazines and newspapers.

It is very easy to spend a great deal of money on stamps, so each collector should decide how much he can afford to spend on his collection, and stick to his budget. Limited funds do not necessarily mean that a collection has to be dull or worthless; a collector who owns many valuable stamps may know so little about philately that his collection has little else to recommend it. On the other hand, a smaller collection may well be so organized and displayed that from a philatelic standpoint it is worth much, much more.

HOW TO ORGANIZE
A STAMP CLUB

Stamp collecting is twice as much fun when you can meet with other collectors to "talk shop" and swap stamps — and there's no better way to do this than to belong to a stamp club. Here you'll be able to increase your knowledge of stamps and exchange your duplicates for stamps you want, while making new friends and participating in many enjoyable activities, both inside and outside of the hobby — stamp auctions, displays, and shows, picnics, excursions, and the like.

There may already be a stamp club established in your neighborhood; if so, you should be able to find out from your local stamp dealer where and when you can attend a meeting, and how you can join. Many schools, churches, libraries, scout troops, YMCA's and YWCA's, and other civic organizations sponsor stamp clubs, too, as a wholesome and worthwhile activity.

Or you can start your own stamp club, with the help of a few friends: just agree to meet together at regular intervals, say, once every other week, to discuss and swap stamps. You can put up notices on your church, school, and shopping center bulletin boards or in stamp dealers' windows, announcing the formation of your club and inviting other collectors to join. If you wish, you can ask one of the civic organizations mentioned above to help you, or to act as your sponsor.

A stamp club can be as formal or informal as you please; it can be simply a group of friends meeting at odd intervals in someone's living room or den. Or it can be a formal organization, with elected officials, a constitution or charter, a club newsletter, a club treasury, and regularly-scheduled meetings in a permanent meeting-place — a room at the public library, church, or school, a basement or garage donated by a member, or perhaps even a rented storefront, complete with philatelic exhibits, literature, and window displays.

You should never forget that the primary purpose c. a stamp club is to have fun, and that official business — reading of secretary's minutes and treasurer's reports, etc. — should be kept to a minimum. Much more time should be allotted to trading sessions where members can sit down and look at each others' collections, discuss items of interest, and exchange duplicates.

There are many different ways you can make your stamp club meetings lively and interesting. From time to time, you might hold a stamp auction, where members put up items for sale to the highest bidder, with a small commission being charged for the benefit of the club treasury. This way, members can dispose profitably of their duplicates, and the club can make some money at the same time.

Occasionally, you might have a guest speaker, the local postmaster, perhaps, or a local collector who is an expert on a certain facet of collecting. Club members, too, can prepare lectures or remarks on their specialties, or other phases of philately. Such speeches and lectures can be great learning opportunities for beginning collectors, and give the more experienced philatelists a chance to display their expertise.

Your club can arrange a get-together with another club, too, for an enjoyable evening of mutual benefit. You'll learn what other collectors are doing, what kinds of activities they are engaged in that your club can try. You can swap stamps with them, often finding items that members of your own club did not have. Your club may even want to collaborate with another club on an exhibition or show, to help gain publicity for the hobby and make new stamp collectors.

This last activity is one of the most important things a stamp club can do — showing other people what stamp collecting is all about, spreading philately, and making new friends for the hobby. At least once a year, your club, either alone or in conjunction with other clubs, should hold an exhibition of your collections in some public place. Perhaps the local library may have some room, or a local merchant may donate space in return for the advertising value; or if you can get enough clubs and collectors together, you can hold a real stamp exhibition in a hall or auditorium.

Interesting displays can be shown, discussing and illustratiing many varieties of a single stamp, for example, or showing how stamps are printed, etc. Especially fine album pages, classic stamps or other desirable issues, stamps and their stories, all make fine exhibits. Prizes should be awarded for the best entry, with local stamp dealers — who will probably be glad to provide the prizes in exchange for the advertising value — acting as judges. Or you can invite an eminent philatelist from a nearby town to act as guest judge.

You should have handbills or notices to distribute to visitors to your exhibition, inviting them to attend a meeting of your club, and encouraging them to start stamp collections of their own. Remember, new members are the lifeblood of a club; a growing membership means bigger and better entertainments, auctions, and activities, more opportunities for swapping duplicates, and more interesting people to meet. The larger your membership, the more interesting and enjoyable your stamp club will be to all who belong to it.

HISTORY OF
FIRST DAY COVERS

If you are a stamp collector, you probably have a few First Day Covers (FDC's) in an album or shoe box. For most collectors an FDC is a cacheted envelope with a new stamp and a First Day of Issue postmark. Some might also have a First Day Program, outlining the Ceremony held on the First Day in the official First Day city.

First Day Cover collecting as we know it today did not start until the 1920's and 30's. Between July, 1922, and Sept. 1923, the first official First Day of Issue, the First Day Ceremony and program, and the first commercial FDC cachet all appeared.

*First use of First Day Issue
cancellation*

It wasn't until 1937 that the familiar "First Day of Issue" slogan was first used. Since then these basic elements of FDC collecting have changed very little.

When considering FDC's before 1922, all the rules change. Collectors accustomed to an official First Day for each new stamp will be surprised to learn there were only nineteen Designated First Days for all US stamps issued before 1922. These official dates were designated by the Post Office in either PO instructions for stamp sale, with the PO announcement of the new issue, or by the Congress in the bill which authorized the stamps.

Even with these few cases, First Day Covers do not exist for all issues with Designated First Days. Often the stamp was not available for sale until after Designated First Day, and in at least one case there is evidence that a stamp sold before the Designated First Day.

"Earliest Dated Cover" without cachet

First Day Covers for most issues before 1922 are more properly called "Earliest Dated Covers". An Earliest Dated Cover is one with the earliest known postmark for the particular issue on cover.

The history of First Day Cover collecting changed when the USPOD designated the first official First Day of Issue on July 12, 1922. This was the First Day of E12, the 10c Special Delivery stamp.

The next stamp issued with an official First Day was the 11c Hayes regular issue, on October 4, 1922, in Washington D.C., and Fremont OH. This FD included several new firsts: the first FD city outside Washington, DC, the FD ceremony and the FD program.

On September 1, 1923, George Linn serviced the first commercially produced US FDC cachet. Linn printed a simple five line cachet on a black bordered, mourning envelope. Several hundred of these cacheted FDC's were

Limprint cachet

prepared and offered for sale in philatelic journals of the period: *Collector's Club Philatelist, Meekel's Weekly Philatelic Gossip,* as well as his own paper, *Linn's Weekly Stamp News.*

From a simple start of one cachet in 1923, cachet making grew in popularity to over thirty different cachets per issue for the Clark and Sullivan commemoratives of 1929, and nearly 100 different cachets per issue for many of the three cent purples of the 1930's.

Cacheted FDC's before 1935 were made in very small quantities and they are getting harder to find every year. Because of this, many collectors are happy to have uncacheted covers in this period.

Cover addressed to Adam Bert

Covers with addresses of prominent FDC enthusiasts, Adam Bert, C.E. Nickles, Henry Hammelman, Philip Ward and Edward Worden are highly sought after by many FDC specialists.

Introduction to Cachet Collecting

Today, many FDC collectors are really cachet collectors. The thrill of the hobby is in finding a scarce cachet for their collection. Up to one hundred different cachets exist for many stamp issues from the mid-1930's up to the present.

Some collectors enjoy the challenge of collecting different cachets for a stamp or a set that they like. Some will collect by topic, such as US history, Masonic history or a professional topic. Topical collections can be researched, written up and mounted on pages to produce a personalized album or exhibit. Others collect by cachet, trying to put together a collection of all the cachets produced by a cachetmaker they like.

CACHETS

Grimsland cachet

ENGRAVED CACHETS have always been very popular with collectors. Four popular engraved cachets are Grimsland, House of Farnam, ArtCraft and Artmaster. Henry Grimsland of Chicago, Illinois produced engraved cachets from 1933 until 1951. Most are one color cachets, with many in the color of the stamp. Most are signed "Grimsland" in the design.

House of Farnam cachets have been produced for every issue from the TIPEX Souvenir sheet of 1936 up to the present. Farnam cachets are engraved usually in one color; many are signed "House of Farnam" or "HF". Since 1970 Farnam has produced two-color cachets.

ArtCraft Cachetts have been continually produced by Washington Stamp Exchange since 1939. The first ArtCraft, prepared for the World's Fair issue of 1939, is an unsigned engraved design, in blue. Most ArtCraft cachets are black, signed with the ArtCraft pallet and brushes trademark.

Artmaster Cachets have been produced for all new U.S. stamps since the Honorable Discharge Commemorative of 1946. Artmaster cachets are engraved cachets, usually in a dark green or gray color, and are signed "Artmaster".

COLORED CACHETS appeal to many FDC collectors. Ioor, Grandy, Staehle and Boll all produced colored cachets. Harry Ioor produced two-colored cachets from 1929 until 1951. In the 1940's and early 50's most Ioor cachets are signed, but before 1940 they are unsigned.

W.M. Grandy produced one or more cachet designs per issue from 1935 until 1957. They are all two color cachets, usually signed "W.M. Grandy", or "WMG".

Ludwig W. Staehel cachet

Ludwig W. Staehle was one of the most prolific US cachet makers, usually producing three or more cachet designs for each issue. Staehle cachets are known for the vivid use of color, often with three or more colors on the design. Staehle produced designs from the late 30's until the early 50's.

Cachet Craft produced cachets from the late 1930's until the early 1970's. During the 1940's Cachet Craft produced attractive two color cachet designs by both L.W. Staehle and Ken Boll. Several popular lines of cachets have been produced from original artwork. C. Stephen Anderson designed cachets from 1933 until his death in 1978. Anderson cachets are usually one color line drawings, with an illustration above, and historical text below. Most are signed "C. Stephen Anderson" or "CSA".

Aristocrat Cachets have been continually produced since 1936. Most Aristocrat cachets will capture the interest of FDC collectors. Fulton, Fluegel, Crosby and "Silk" cachets are very popular for these reasons.

Fulton cachet

Fulton Cachets are finely engraved cachets, usually printed in color rather than black. Because Fultons were produced only from 1947 to 1950, they offer an opportunity to assemble a complete collection of very attractive cachets. While many Fultons can be located with some persistence, a few, such as the foreign issues and the US Utah cachet, are quite difficult to find.

House of Farnam cachet

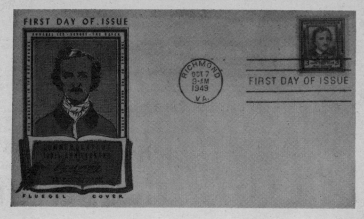

Fluegel cachet

Fluegel Covers are attractive multicolored cachets produced from 1945 until 1968. Attractive use of color is being appreciated more and more by the cachet collector, and all Fluegel cachets are becoming harder and harder to find.

Crosby cachet

One of the most intriguing cachetmakers of the 1930's and 40's is W.G. Crosby. Crosby produced cachets using a raised print, with a space in the printed design for a small photo to be posted on the cover. Crosby produced many varieties of his cachet by changing the printed design and the photo. Over twenty five different Crosby cachet varieties are known to exist on the Navy issue of 1945.

"Silk" Cachets have been produced in the United States only since 1971. However, since that time, they have

"Silk" cachet

become the most popular and fastest growing cachet on the market. As new collectors have gone back to buy the early "Silk" Cachets, the demand has far exceeded the supply. Today many early "Silk" Cachets are bringing high prices when they appear on the market.

Another very popular area of FDC collecting is First Cachets. A First Cachet is the very first cachet produced by any cachetmaker. Very often the first cachets were produced in small quantities. First cachets by the popular cachetmakers such as ArtCraft, Colorano, Farnam, Fluegel, Fulton and others are difficult to locate and sell for ten to fifty times the price of a common cachet on the same issue.

ACCESSORIES

STAMP TONGS

To avoid getting your stamps soiled or creased, you should never handle them with you fingers, or with anything other than a clean pair of good quality stamp tongs. These handy tweezer-like instruments are easy to use, and come in several different styles, allowing you to choose according to your own personal preference. A good pair of stamp tongs should be thin enough to pick a stamp up from a flat surface, and should have slightly rounded ends and highly polished edges and surfaces to avoid damaging the stamp.

PERFORATION GAUGE

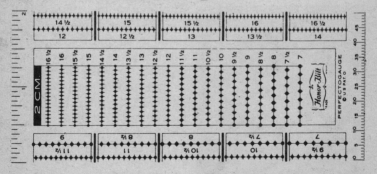

Measuring the number of perforation holes in a two-centimeter space along the edge of a stamp is often the only way to tell the difference between two stamps that may look exactly alike, but actually belong to different issues. By placing a stamp on a perforation gauge, and moving the stamp up and down until the dots on the gauge perfectly fit the holes along the edge of the stamp, you can tell exactly what the "perf. number" is.

MAGNIFIERS

Magnifying glasses enable you to examine stamps closely and identify details too small to be seen easily with the naked eye. Magnifiers come in many different styles, ranging from small, folding pocket magnifiers to large battery-powered "flashlight" types and stand-type magnifiers which leave both hands free.

WATERMARK TRAY & FLUID

Watermarks on stamps (see pg. 126) are often very difficult to see clearly, so stamp collectors use various methods to make them easier to detect. The most common method is to place the stamp face down in a black tray or dish and pour a few drops of detector fluid onto the stamp, making the watermarked design stand out against the black background.

CAUTION: Watermark detection fluids may react unfavorably with some inks and dissolve them, so extreme care should be taken in their use.

STAMP LIFT

The stamplift is a non-chemical device used to remove old hinges and separate stuck-together or stuck-down mint stamps without destroying the original gum.

UV LAMP

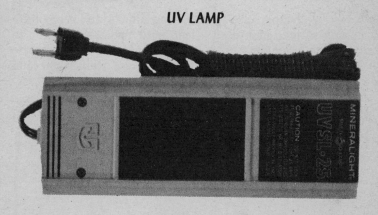

Ultraviolet lamps are used to make phosphor tags (see pg. 151) visible, and can be obtained either as complete units, or as ultraviolet bulbs which will fit into regular fluorescent or incandescent fixtures. Direct ultraviolet light can damage the eyes, so you should take care not to look directly into an ultraviolet lamp;.

STAMP PRESS

A stamp press is used to flatten out folds and creases in stamps, and to prevent them from curling while they are drying after having been soaked.

GLASSINE ENVELOPES

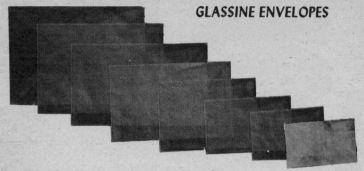

Many collectors use glassine envelopes to keep their stamps sorted, identified, clean, and undamaged prior to mounting them in an album, or to package and prepare them for sale or trading. Glassines are translucent and come in a wide range of sizes.

STOCK BOOKS

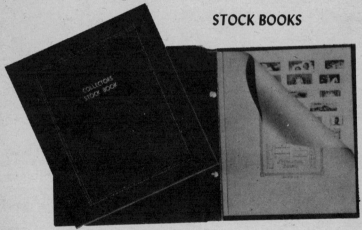

Stock books are temporary albums used to keep stamps for preliminary sorting or accumulation prior to mounting, or to keep duplicates for sale or trade. The pages have long, shallow pockets into which stamps can be slipped; they are then held reasonably secure, but can be quickly and easily removed when necessary. Stock books may have either stiff manila pocket pages or transparent plastic pockets on black backing, to show off your stamps better; they may be inexpensive, and small enough to fit into your pocket or purse, or as large and luxurious as any standard stamp album.

HINGES

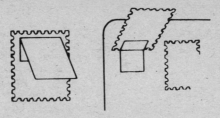

Stamp Hinges are small pieces of gummed glassine paper used to mount stamps in your album. The shiny side is gummed; keep it outside as you fold the hinge.

Just moisten the upper half of the gummed side of the hinge and attach it to the back of the stamp; then moisten the other half and attach it to the album page. It's easy! (Remember to leave the stamp, where it is hinged in the album, until dry; otherwise if you try to remove the stamp, you may damage it.)

MOUNTS

1. Insert stamp in tube.
2. Trim tube close to stamp with scissors.
3. Moisten gum, and fasten to album.
4. Fold back upper part of tube and crease so stamp will lie flat.
5. Crystal Mount eliminates hinges, for fold at the top serves as a hinge.

Another method of mounting stamps in an album is to use plastic strips or tubes, which can be cut to an exact fit. Stamps thus mounted are well-protected by the tough plastic shell, but remain completely visible. Use of plastic mounts instead of hinges also means that the original gum on mint stamps remains intact. There are many different mounts available, including Crystal Mount, made in the U.S.A.

CATALOGUES

A catalogue is basically an illustrated list of stamps, usually arranged in sets according to face value, and listed in order of the date of issue. Besides helping to identify stamps and giving the current market values, catalogues also provide other information: color and design variations, watermarks, perforation numbers, type of printing used, etc. Both general world-wide and specialized catalogues are available.

WORLD-WIDE CATALOGUES

The world-wide catalogue most widely used in the United States is the Scott Standard Postage Stamp Catalogue (U.S.). Other highly regarded world-wide catalogues include the Minkus (U.S.), Stanley Gibbons (Great Britain), Michel (Germany), and Yvert & Tellier (France).

In the catalogues the individual stamps in the set are listed, with the index, or catalogue, number, design-type number (referring to the illustration with that number), denomination, color (if two or more colors are used, the color of the

HOW TO COLLECT STAMPS

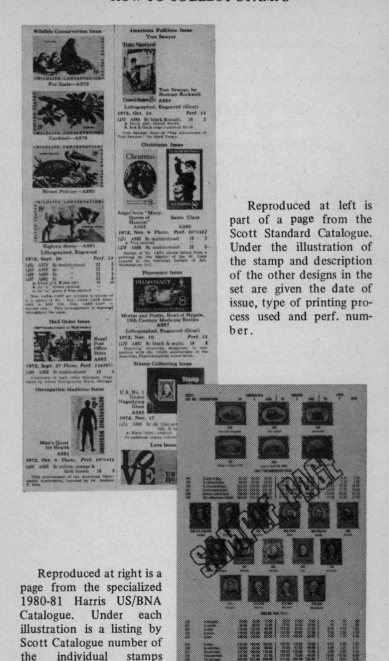

Reproduced at left is part of a page from the Scott Standard Catalogue. Under the illustration of the stamp and description of the other designs in the set are given the date of issue, type of printing process used and perf. number.

Reproduced at right is a page from the specialized 1980-81 Harris US/BNA Catalogue. Under each illustration is a listing by Scott Catalogue number of the individual stamps having that design.

frame or border is given first, then the colors of the central, or vignette portion of the design), and the prices for unused and cancelled copies of the stamp. Minor variations are denoted by a lowercase alphabet letter.

SPECIALIZED CATALOGUES

Specialized catalogues deal with specific topics, countries, or types of issues. The largest selling catalog for U.S. and Canada stamps is the Harris Reference Catalog of Postage Stamp Prices of the United States, United Nations, Canada & Provinces. Other prominent specialized catalogues include the Scott U.S. Specialized Catalogue, Sanabria's World Airmail Catalogue (for collectors who specialize in airmail issues), and many country and regional catalogues. It is also possible to get listings of issues on specific topics from some of the topical collecting societies.

ALBUMS

The best way to keep your stamp collection organized, well-protected, and beautifully displayed is to mount your stamps in an album.

In choosing an album, consider carefully your own interests and needs — are you interested in collecting stamps from around the world, or from one specific country; or are you interested in a specific topic, like sports or flowers, or a specific type of stamp, like air mails or special deliveries? Whatever your interests, albums come in such a wide range of classes, prices, sizes and types that there is bound to be one that is just right for you.

One thing to remember when buying an album: experienced collectors everywhere agree that you should always get the largest album you can possibly afford. A small album will run out of pages and space and become badly overcrowded almost before you know it. Then you may be faced with the unpleasant task of removing all of your stamps from your old album and remounting them in a new one. The larger your stamp album, the less likelihood there is that you will run out of space.

Loose-leaf albums, especially, are virtually a must because they allow you to add or rearrange pages whenever if becomes necessary. Most album manufacturers publish annual supplements for their loose-leaf albums, allowing you to keep your collection up-to-date with the latest issues.

There are two general classes of albums, those in which the pages have ruled spaces for the stamps (often illustrated), and those in which the pages are blank. Within the ruled-space category one finds the general world-wide albums, plus most single-country specialized albums; blank albums are generally for collectors with very specialized interests, or very advanced collectors who wish to design their own albums.

World-wide albums can range in size and comprehensiveness from the very smallest beginner's album costing about $1.00 to the huge 8-Volume International, costing more than $700.00. The larger the album, of course, the more complete it will be, but all world-wide albums, regardless of size, are by necessity abridged to some degree. To be truly complete, an album would have to include every stamp ever issued by every country in the world since Great Britain issued the first adhesive postage stamp, the famous "Penny Black", back in 1840. This would not only require many, many volumes, but would also mean providing spaces for many rare stamps which are today essentially unobtainable to all but the very wealthiest collectors — if they are obtainable at all. The most popular world-wide albums today are those which concentrate on the easily-obtainable low-and medium-priced stamps which the average collector is most likely to have in abundance.

Specialized albums concentrate on stamps from specific areas — individual countries, like the United States or France, or groups of countries, like the British Commonwealth; individual topics, like sports, space, or flowers; and individual types of issues, like airmails, special deliveries, or postage dues, Individual country albums usually have spaced and illustrated pages; other specialty albums usually have blank pages with simple titles.

Some excellent examples of specialized single-country albums, all loose-leaf, are pictured here. The U.S. Liberty Album is 100% illustrated and virtually complete for issues of the United States, U.S. Possessions, and Confederate States, It includes not only regular postage and air mails, but also special deliveries, postage dues, cut squares, revenues, hunting stamps, etc. For beginning U.S. collectors, the Independence Album offers many of the same features as the larger, much more comprehensive Liberty, with spaces for more than 1,100 stamps, 100% illustrated. The 2-Volume U.S. Plate Block Album is 100% illustrated, and is specifically designed for collectors of United States plate blocks or ordinary blocks of 4.

The Canada & Provinces Album is 100% complete and 100% illustrated for Canada, British Columbia & Vancouver Island, New Brunswick, Newfoundland, Nova Scotia & Prince Edward Island. The United States Classic is the most complete, 100% illustrated U. S. Album in the history of printed albums and at a truly reasonable price. The Germany album is a beautifully-designed volume for collectors who specialize in the stamps of this philatelically very popular country, while the Soviet Republics album is a fine example of a specialty album for a logically collectible group of countries, in this case the individual states which make up the Union of Soviet Socialist Republics (U.S.S.R.).

Blank albums are primarily for collectors who cannot find exactly what they want in a standard ruled-space album, or who want to arrange their stamps themselves, rather than mount them according to a pre-arranged order or pattern. They are particularly suitable for topical collectors.

The pages themselves may be entirely blank, or they may have a faint blue or gray quadrille-type ruled background, to help the collector arrange the stamps in a balanced pattern. The ruling may be standard 1/4, 1/5., or 1/8-inch squares; also available are the Harris "Speed-rille" ruled pages, which have faint gray lines dividing the pages into various equal sections — fifths, sixths, sevenths, etc. — to make it easier to evenly space out a row of of stamps.

Often, the pages will also have decorative ruled borders, and may come with separate printed titles which are gummed and may be affixed to the pages as the collector desires. In the case of blank albums designed for specific topics or countries, the pages may not only have decorative ruled borders, they may also have fancy titles and illustrations.

Blank albums for topical collections will usually come in matched sets of binder and pages, with extra pages available separately; but you can also select a binder and pages separately, to suit your own taste. There is a wide variety of binders available, in different sizes and of different constructions, as well as many different styles and sizes of blank pages.

If you decide to mount your collection in a blank album, some accessories you may find helpful are: a stamp positioner to help you space out your stamps on non-ruled pages; stencil guides, for writing descriptive captions for the stamps; and decorative gummed flags and coat-of-arms of various countries and states, to add a colorfully attractive touch to your blank pages.

Special albums are also available for collectors of first day covers and mint sheets. Cover albums have cover-sized transparent plastic pockets into which the covers are slipped, while mint sheet albums have whole pages made of sheets of plastic, open at the top and one side, and closed at the bottom and the binder side, so the sheets can easily be inserted and removed, yet will not fall out.

Most of the larger stamp companies today produce large, highly illustrated supply catalogues and would be pleased to send you their latest catalogue and fascinating world-wide stamps for your approval.

WORLD-WIDE STAMP IDENTIFIER

By picking out a word, sign or symbol on a stamp of unknown origin and looking it up in the index, the collector will be guided at once, in most cases, to the stamp's correct country name.

Only the relatively difficult-to-classify stamps have been indexed. If the country name in its English form appears anywhere on the stamp, no identifying words are necessary and none have been included here.

Likewise, such words as "postage" and "pence," for example, which appear on the stamps of dozens of countries, would be of little or no value as guides. For this reason, *if you do not find the first words you look up, try other words on the stamp* until the indexing word is found.

Some stamps — early Afghanistan and Egypt, certain of the Indian Native States, and others — are printed entirely in Arabic or other Oriental characters and therefore cannot be indexed. To help you with these stamps, see the illustrated section, "OTHER HARD-TO-IDENTIFY STAMPS" at the end of the regular listings.

A

A. B. on stamps of Russia: **Far Eastern Republic.**

АВИОПОУТА: Russia.

A.C.C.P.: Azerbaijan.

AÇORES: Azores.

A.D. HALL: United States – Gainsville, Alabama.

A.E.F. ("Afrique Equatoriale Francaise") on stamps inscribed
         "Centenaire du Gabon": **French Equatorial Africa.**

ΛΕΓΤΑ: Greece.

ΛΕΗΤΑ: Epirus.

AFGAN, AFGHANES: Afghanistan.

AFRICA CORREIOS: Portuguese Africa.

AFRICA OCCIDENTAL ESPAÑOLA: Spanish West Africa.

AFRICA ORIENTALE ITALIANA: Italian East Africa.

AFRIQUE EQUATORIAL FRANÇAISE: French Equatorial Africa;
on stamps inscribed "Moyen Congo": **Middle Congo**;
plus "Tchad": **Chad**; With bars through "Gabon"
and value: **French Equatorial Africa**; on stamps of
Gabon: **Gabon.**

AFRIQUE EQUATORIALE GABON: Gabon.

AFRIQUE OCCIDENTALE FRANÇAISE: French West Africa.

ΛΗΜΝΟΣ on stamps of Greece: **Greece – Aegean Islands – Lemnos.**

AITUTAKI on stamps of New Zealand or Cook Islands: **Aitukaki.**

ALAOUITES on stamps of France and Syria: **Alaouites.**

ALBANIA on stamps of Italy: **Italy – Offices in Turkey – Albania.**

ALBANY GA.: United States – Albany, Georgia.

ALECHA on stamps of Peru: **Peru – Ancachs**

ALEXANDRIA: United States – Alexandria, Virginia.

ALEXANDRIE: France – Offices in Egypt – Alexandria.

ALGERIE on stamps of France: **Algeria.**

ALLEMAGNE DUITSCHLAND on stamps of Belgium: **Germany – Belgian occupation.**

A.M.G.–F.T.T. on stamps of Italy: **Trieste – Zone A.**

A.M.G.–V.G. on stamps of Italy: **Italy – Venezia Giulia – Allied occupation.**

A.M. POST: Germany – Allied occupation.

ANDERSON C. H. S.C.: United States – Anderson Court House, South Carolina.

ANDORRA on stamps of Spain: **Andorra – Spanish Administration.**

ANDORRE on stamps of France: **Andorra – French Administration.**

ANNA: British East Africa, India, Indian States, Mesopotamia, Pakistan, Zanzibar.

ANNAPOLIS: United States – Annapolis, Maryland.

ANTIOQUIA: Colombia – Antioquia.

A.O. on stamps of Congo Democratic Republic (ex-Belgian): **German East Africa.**

A.O.F. on stamps of France: **French West Africa.**

A.O.I. on stamps of Italy: **Italian East Africa.**

A PAYER TE BETALEN ("postage due"): **Belgium.**

A PERÇEVOIR: Belgium, France, many **French Colonies.**

APURIMAC on stamps inscribed "Franqued": **Peru – Apurimac.**

АРЖАВА: Jugoslavia.

A.R.: Colombia, Montenegro, Panama, Chile.

ARABIE SAOUDITE: Saudi Arabia.

ARCHIPEL DES COMORES: Comoro Islands, Grand Comoro.

A RECEMBER: Portugal, Portuguese Colonies.

ARRIBA on stamps of Spain: **Spain — San Sebastian.**

ASCENSION on stamps of St. Helena: **Ascension.**

ASSISTENCIA D.L. on 72 on war tax stamps of Portuguese India:
Timor.

ATHENS S.A.: United States — Athens, Georgia.

ATLANTA GA. or **GEO.**: United States — Atlanta, Georgia.

ATT, ATTS: Siam

A & T on stamps of French Colonies: **Annam and Tonkin.**

AUNUS: on stamps of Finland: **Russia — Finnish occupation.**

AUR: Iceland.

AUSTIN, MISS.: United States — Austin, Mississippi.

AUSTIN, TEX.: United States — Austin, Texas.

AUSTRALIAN ANTARCTIC TERRITORY: Australia — Australian Antarctic
Territory.

AVISPORTO: Denmark.

AVO, AVOS: Macao, Timor.

A.W. McNEEL P.M.: United States — Autaugaville, Alabama.

AYACUCHO: Peru — Ayacucho.

ΑΥΤΟΝΟΜΟΣ: Epirus.

AZERBAIDJAN: Azerbaijan.

B

B in an oval, on stamps with no country name: **Belgium —**
parcel post stamps; on stamps of Straits Settlements:
Bangkok.

BADEN: Germany — Baden — French occupation.

B.A. ERITREA, B.A. SOMALIA, or **B.A. TRIPOLITANIA** on stamps
of Great Britain: **Great Britain — Offices in Africa —
Eritrea, Somalia, Tripolitania.**

BAGHDAD on stamps of Turkey: **Mesopotamia.**

BAHAWALPUR: Pakistan — Bahawalpur.

BAHRAIN: on stamps of Great Britain or India: **Bahrain**

BAHT: Siam.

БАНДЕРОЛЬНОЕ ОТУРАВЛЕНИЕ: Russia — Offices in Turkey.

BAJAR PORTO: Indonesia.

BAMRA: India — Bamra.

BÁNÁT BÁCSKA on stamps of Hungary: **Hungary — Serbian occupation —
Banata, Bacaska.**

BANI: Romania; on stamps of Austria: **Romania — Austrian occupation.**

BARANYA on stamps of Hungary: **Hungary — Serbian occupation.**

BARBUDA on stamps of Antigua or Leeward Islands: **Barbuda.**

BARCELONA: Spain.

BARWANI: India – Barwani.

BASEL: Switzerland – Basel.

BASUTOLAND on stamps of South Africa: **Basutoland.**

BATAAN on stamps with inscriptions in oriental characters:
Philippines – **Japanese occupation.**

BATON ROUGE, LA.: United States – Baton Rouge, Louisiana.

БАТУМ. ОБ., БАТУМОБЯАС, БАТУМСКАЯ ПОЧТА, БАТУМБОБЛ on
stamps of Russia: **Batum**

BAYERN, BAYR: Bavaria.

B.C.A. on stamps inscribed "British South Africa Company":
British Central Africa.

B.C.M., BRITISH CONSULAR MAIL: Madagascar – British Consulate.

B.C.O.F.–JAPAN 1946 on stamps of Australia: **Australia.**

B. DPTO. ZELAYA: Nicaragua – Zelaya.

BEAUMONT: United States – Beaumont, Texas.

BECHUANLAND on stamps of South Africa: **Becuanaland.**

BECHUANALAND PROTECTORATE on stamps of Great Britain: **Bechuanaland
Protectorate.**

ВЕНДЕНСКАЯ: Russia – Wenden.

BELGIAN EAST AFRICA: Ruanda-Urundi.

BELGIE: Belgium.

BELGIEN on stamps of Germany: **Belgium – German occupation**

BELGIQUE: Belgium.

BELGISCH CONGO: Belgian Congo

BELIZE: British Honduras.

BENADIR: Somalia.

BENGASI on stamps of Italy: **Italy – Offices in Africa – Bengasi.**

BENIN on stamps of French Colonies: **Benin.**

BERLIN on stamps of Germany: **Germany – Berlin.**

BEYROUTH on stamps of Russia: **Russia – Offices in Turkey.**

BHOPAL: India – Bhopal.

BHOR: India – Bhor.

BIAFRA on stamps of Nigeria: issued by revolutionary forces in 1968-69.

B.I.O.T. on stamps of Seychelles: **British Indian Ocean Territory.**

BISHOP'S: United States – Cleveland, Ohio.

B.M.A. ERITREA, B.M.A. SOMALIA, or B.M.A. TRIPOLITANIA on
stamps of Great Britain: **Great Britain – Offices
in Africa – Eritrea, Somalia, or Tripolitania.**

BMA MALAYA: Straits Settlements

ВОСТОЧНАЯ КОРРЕСПОНДЕНЦIЯ: Russia – Offices in Turkey.

BOFTGEBIET on stamps of Germany: **Lithuania – German occupation**

BOGCHAN, BOGACHES: Yemen.

BÖHMEN ÛND MÄHREN: Czechoslovakia – Bohemia and Moravia.

BOHΘEITE: Greece.

BOLIVAR: Colombia – Bolivar.

BOLLODELLA DI SICINA: Two Sicilies – Sicily.

BOLLO POSTALE: San Marino.

BOSNIEN-HERAEGOVINA or **BOSNIEIHERZEGOWINA:** Bosnia and
         Herzegovina.

BOŸACA: Colombia – Boyaca.

BRASIL: Brazil.

BRATTLEBORO VT.: United States – Brattleboro, Vermont.

BRAUNSCHWIG: Brunswick.

BRIEFPOST: Germany – French occupation.

BRITISH BECUANALAND on stamps of Cape of Good Hope or Great
         Britain: **Becuanaland.**

BRITISH EAST AFRICA COMPANY on stamps of Great Britain:
         British East Africa.

BRITISH NEW GUINEA: Papua New Guinea.

BRITISH OCCUPATION on stamps of Russia: **Batum.**

BRITISH PROTECTORATE OIL RIVERS on stamps of Great Britain:
         Niger Coast Protectorate.

BRITISH SOMALILAND on stamps of India: **Somaliland Protectorate.**

BRITISH SOUTH AFRICA COMPANY: Rhodesia.

BRITISH VICE CONSULATE: Madagascar – British Consulate.

BR. or **BRITISH VIRGIN ISLANDS**: Virgin Islands.

BROWN & McOILLS: United States – Lousiville, Kentucky.

BRUNEI on stamps of Labuan: **Brunei.**

BRUXELLES, BRUSSEL: Belgium.

BUENOS ARIES: Argentina – Buenos Aires; with "Agosto de 1921":
         Argentina.

BUITEN BEZIT on stamps inscribed "Nederlandsch-Indie": **Dutch**
         Indies.

BULGARIE: Bulgaria.

BUNDI: India – Bundi.

BURMA on stamps of India: **Burma.**

BUSHIRE on stamps of Persia: **Bushire.**

BUSSAHIR: India – Bussahir.

C

C preceded by numeral of value, on stamps with Japanese characters:
         Ryukyu Islands.

CABO: Nicaragua – Cabo Graclas a Dios.

HOW TO COLLECT STAMPS

CABO JUBI, CABO JUBY on stamps of Rio de Oro, Spain, or Spanish Morocco: **Cape Juby.**

CABO VERDE: Cape Verde.

CACHES on stamps of France or French Colonies: **French India.**

CADIZ on stamps of Spain: **Spain – Cadiz.**

САНАТОРИУМЬ: Bulgaria.

CAIMO: Puerto Rico – Caimo.

CALCHI on stamps of Italy: **Italy – Aegean Islands – Calchi.**

CALIMNO or **CALINO** on stamps of Italy: **Italy – Calimno.**

CAMBODGE: Cambodia.

CAMEROONS U.K.T.T. on stamps of Nigeria: (British) **Cameroons.**

CAMEROUN on stamps of Gabon or Middle Congo: **Cameroun.**

CAMPECHE: Mexico – Campeche.

CAMPIONARIA DE TRIPOLI: Tripolitania, Libya.

CANAL ZONE on stamps of Colombia, Panama, or United States: **Canal Zone.**

CANARIAS on stamps of Spain: **Spain – Canary Islands.**

CANTON on stamps of Indo-China: **France – Offices in China – Canton.**

CARCHI on stamps of Italy: **Italy – Aegean Islands – Karki.**

CARRIERS: United States – Provisional Issues.

CASO on stamps of Italy: **Italy – Aegean Islands – Caso.**

CASTELLORISO, CASTELLORIZO or **CASTELLOROSSO** on stamps of France, French Colonies, or Italy: **Castellorizo.**

CAUCA: Colombia – Cauca.

CAVALLE: France – Offices in Turkey – Cavalle.

C C C P (Abbreviation for "Union of Soviet Socialist Republics"): **Russia.**

C. CH. on stamps of French Colonies: **Cochin China.**

C. or **CS. DE PESO: Philippines.**

CECHY A MORAVA: Czechoslovakia – Bohemia and Moravia.

C. E. F. (Cameroon Expeditionary Force) on stamps inscribed "Kamerun":(British) **Cameroons;** (Chinese Expeditionary Force) on stamps of India: **India** – military stamps.

CENT or **CENTS** on stamps of France: **France – Offices in China;** on stamps of Russia: **Russia – Offices in China;** with crowns in a circle: **Mongolia.**

CENTENAIRE ALGERIE ("Algerian Centenary"): **France.**

CENTENAIRE DU GABON: French Equatorial Africa.

CENTESIMI: Italy, many Italian Colonies, **San Marino, Vatican City;** on stamps of Austria or Bosnia and Herzegovina: **Italy – Austrian occupation.**

CENTESIMI DI CORONA in serif letters on stamps of Italy: **Austria –
Italian occupation;** in sans-serif letters on stamps of
Italy: **Dalmatia.**

CENTIMES on stamps of Germany: **Germany – Offices in Turkey;**
on stamps of Austria: **Austria – Offices in Crete.**

CENTIMOS with no country name: **Spain;** on stamps of France:
French Morocco.

CESKOSLOVENSKA, ČESKOSLOVENSKO: Czechoslovakia.

CESKO-SLOVENSKO: Czechoslovakia – Slovakia.

C F A on stamps of France: **Reunion.**

C. G. H. S.: Upper Silesia.

CH followed by oriental characters: **Korea.**

CHALA: Peru – Chala.

CHAMBA: India – Chamba.

CHAPEL HILL N.C.: United States – Chapel Hill, North Carolina.

CHARKHARI: India – Charkhari.

CHARLESTON S.C.: United States – Charleston, South Carolina.

CHATTANOOGA, TEN.: United States – Chattanooga, Tennessee.

CHEMINS DE FER SPOORWEGEN: Belgium.

CHIFFRE TAXE with no country name: **France, French Colonies.**

CHINA on stamps of Hong Kong: **Great Britain – Offices in
China;** on stamps of Germany: **Germany – Offices in
China.**

CHINE on stamps of France: **France – Offices in China.**

CHRISTMAS ISLAND on stamps of Australia: **Christmas Island.**

CIHS on stamps of Germany: **Upper Silesia.**

CILICIE on stamps of France or Turkey: **Cilicia.**

CINQUANTENAIRE 24 SEPTEMBRE on postage due stamps of French
Colonies: **New Caledonia** – postage due stamps.

CIRENNICA on stamps of Italy or Tripolitania: **Cyrenaica.**

CITY DISPATCH POST: United States – New York, New York.

CITY POST: United States – Charleston, South Carolina.

C.M.T. on stamps of Austria: **Western Ukrain – Romanian occupation.**

CN (for "cheun"): **Korea.**

COCHIN, COCHIN ANCHAL: India – Cochin.

CO. Ci. on stamps of Jugoslavia: **Jugoslavia – Ljubljana.**

COLIS POSTAL or **POSTAUX** on stamps with no country name:
Belgium.

COLOMBIA on stamps showing a map of Panama: **Panama – Colombian
dominon.**

COLONIA DE RIO DE ORO: Rio de Oro.

COLONIA ERITREA on stamps of Italy or Somalia: **Eritrea.**

COLONIE or **COLOLIALI ITALIANE: Italian Colonies.**

COLONIES DEL'EMPIRE FRANCAISE: French Colonies.

COLONIES POSTES: French Colonies.

COLUMBIA plus **P.O.** or **POST OFFICE:** United States – Columbia, South Carolina.

COLUMBIA TEN.: United States – Columbia, Tennessee.

COLUMBUS, GA.: United States – Columbus, Georgia.

COMANHIA DO NYASSA ("Nyassa Company"): Nyassa.

COMITE FRANAIS DE LA LIBERATION NATIONAL: French Colonies.

COMMISSION DE GOUVERNEMENT HAUTE SILESIE: Upper Silesia.

COMMISSON INTERALLIEE MARIENWERDER on stamps of Germany: Marienwerder.

COMORES: Comoro Islands.

COMP. or **COMPANHIA DE MOÇAMBIQUE:** Mozambique Company: on stamps of Mozambique: **Mozambique Company.**

COMUNICAÇIONES: Spain.

CONFEDERATE STATES or **CONFEDERATE STATES OF AMERICA:** United States – Confederate States.

CONFEDERATO HELVETICA ("Helvetic Confederation"): Switzerland.

CONGO on stamps with Portuguese inscriptions: **Portuguese Congo;** with "Belge": **Congo Democratic Republic** (ex-Belgian); with "Francaise": **French Congo;** with "Francaise Gabon": **Gabon;** with "Republique du": **Congo Democratic Republic** (ex-Belgian) or **Congo People's Republic** (ex-French).

CONGRESO DE LOS DIPUTADOS: Spain.

CONSTANTINOPLE on stamps of Russia: **Russia – Offices in Turkey.**

CONSTANTINOPOLI on stamps of Italy: **Italy – Offices in Turkey – Constantinople.**

COO on stamps of Italy: **Italy – Aegean Islands – Coo.**

COOK ISLANDS – NIUE: Niue.

CORDOBA: Argentina – Croboda.

COREE, COREAN: Korea.

CORFU on stamps of Greece or Italy: **Corfu – Italian occupation.**

CORONA: Dalmatia; on stamps of Italy: **Austria – Italian occupation.**

CORREIO with no country name: **Portugal.**

CORREO AEREO with no country name: **Spain.**

CORREO ESPAÑOL MARRUECOS on stamps of Spain: **Spanish Morocco.**

CORREO ESPAÑOL TANGER: Spanish Morocco – Tangier.

CORREO URBANO DE BOGOTA: Colombia – Bogota.

CORREOS with no country name and denomination in CUATOS, REALES, CS, or CTOS., (i.e., CENTIMOS): **Spain;** with "Real": **Dominican Republic.**

CORREOS with no country name: **Cuba, Peru, Philippines, Dominican Republic, Spain, Uruguay.**

CORREOS ARGENTINOS: Argentina.

CORREOS DE COLOMBIA: Colombia.

CORREIOS, CORREIOS E TELEGRAPHOS: Portugal.

CORREOS INTERRIOR: Philippines.

CORREOS MEXICO GOBIERNO REVOLUCIONARO: Mexico – Yeatan.

CORREOS NAÇIONALES: Colombia.

CORREOS NALES: Colombia.

CORREOS OXACA: Mexico – Oaxaca.

CORREOS SONORA: Mexico – Sonora.

CORREOS Y TELEGs: Spain.

CORRESPONDENCIA URGENTE: Spain.

CORRIENTES: Argentina – Corrientes.

COS on stamps of Italy: **Italy – Aegean Islands – Coo.**

COSTA ATLANTICA B: Nicaragua – Zeleya.

COSTA ATLANTICA C: Nicaragua – Cabo Gracias a Dios.

COTE DE SOMALIS or **COTE FRANÇAIS: Somali Coast.**

COTE D'IVOIRE: Ivory Coast.

COURTLAND AL: United States – Courtland, Alabama.

СРБИЈА: Serbia.

СРБСКА: Serbia.

CRUZ ROJA DOMINICANA: Dominican Republic.

CRUZ ROJA HONDURENA: Honduras.

CRVENI KRST on stamps of Jugoslavia; **Jugoslavia – Offices Abroad, Montenegro – German occupation.**

CROISSANT ROUGE TURC: Turkey.

CRUZ VERMELHA PORTUGUESA: Portugal.

C.S. or **C.S. A. POSTAGE: United States – Confederate States.**

СТ., СТОТ., СТОТИНКИ: Bulgaria.

CUAUTLA: Mexico – Cuantla.

CUBA on stamps of United States: **Cuba – U.S. Administration**

CUERNAVACA: Mexico – Cuernavaca.

CUNDINAMARCA: Colombia – Cundinamarca.

CURAÇAO: Netherlands Antilles.

CUZCO on stamps inscribed "Peru" or "Franqued": **Peru – Cuzco.**

C.X.C. ("Serbs, Croats, and Slovenes"): **Jugoslavia.**

CYPRUS on stamps of Great Britain: **Cyprus.**

D

D (for "dinar") on stamps with Arabic writing: **Persia.**

d (pence), **/** (shilling) or **£** (pound) preceded by a numeral,
on stamps with king or queen's head but no country
name: **Great Britain.**

d/ on stamps of Cape of Good Hope: **Griqualand West.**

DAI NIPPON on stamps of Straits Settlements: **Malaya – Japanese
occupation;** on various Malaya States: **Malaya States –
Japanese occupation** – of state overprinted on.

DALTON GA.: United States – Dalton, Georgia.

DANMARK: Denmark.

DANSK-VESTINDISKE or **VESTINDIEN: Danish West Indies.**

DANVILLE, VA.: United States – Danville, Virginia.

DANZIG on stamps of Germany: **Danzig.**

DARDANELLES on stamps of Russia: **Russia – Offices in Turkey.**

D.B.L. in script letters on stamps of Russia: **Far Eastern
Republic;** with three bars: **Siberia.**

DDR: Germany – German Democratic Republic.

DEDDAHG: France – Offices in Turkey.

DEFICIT: Peru.

DELEGACOES: Portugal.

DEL GOLFO DE GUINEA: Spanish Guinea.

DENWAISEN SIROTAM on stamps of Italy: **Jugoslavia – Ljublana –
German occupation.**

DEUTFCHES REICH on stamps of Bavaria: **Bavaria.**

DEUTFCHES REICH: Germany.

DEUTFCHÖFTERREICH: Austria.

DEUTSCHLAND: Germany – Allied occupation.

DEUTSCH: ("German") followed by **NEU-GUINEA: German New Guinea;**
by **OSTAFRIKA: German East Africa;** by **SÜDWESTAFRIKA:
German South West Africa.**

**DEUTSCH DEMOKRATISCHE REPUBLIK: Germany – German Democratic
Republic.**

DEUTSCHE BUNDESPOST: Germany; inscribed **BERLIN: Germany – Berlin.**

DEUTSCHE FELDPOST: Germany – military parcel post stamps.

DEUTSCHE MILITAER-VERWALLUNG MONTENEGRO on stamps
of Jugoslavia:
Montenegro – German occupation.

DEUTSCHE NATIONAL VERSAMMLUNG: Germany.

DEUTSCHE POFT or **POST: Germany, Germany – Berlin, Germany –
German Democratic Republic.**

DEUTSCHES POST OSTEN on stamps of Germany: **Poland – German occupation.**

DEUTSCHES REICH: Germany.

**DEUTSCHES REICH GENERALGOUVERNEMENT: Poland – German
occupation.**

DEUTSCHES REICHS-POST: Germany.

DHAR: India – Dhar.

D.H. GHASS P.M.: United States – Lynchburg, Virgina.

DIEGO-SUAREZ on stamps of French Colonies: **Diego-Suarez.**

DIENST on stamps inscribed "Nederlandsch-Indie": **Dutch Indies.**

DIENSTMARKE: Bavaria, Danzig, Germany, Prussia, Saar.

DIENST SACHE: Wurttenberg – Official stamps.

DILIGENCIA: Uruguay.

DINAR or **DINARS:** Persia.

DINERO: Peru.

DIOS, PATRIA, REY: Spain.

DISTRITO: Peru – Cuzco.

DJ or **DJIBOUTI** on stamps of Obock: **Somali Coast.**

DOLLAR on stamps of Russia: **Russia – Offices in China.**

DOLLATA: Central Lithuania, Poland.

DOPLATIT or **DOPLATNE** with no country name: **Czechoslovakia.**

DRZAVA, DRZAVNA on stamps of Bosnia and Herzegovina: **Jugoslavia – Bosnia and Herzegovina.**

DUC. DL. PARMA: Parma.

DUITSCH OOST AFRIKA BELGISCHE BEZETTING on stamps of Congo Democratic Republic (ex-Belgian): **German East Africa – Belgian occupation.**

DURAZZO on stamps of Italy: **Italy – Offices in Turkey – Durazzo.**

DUTTIA: India – Duttia.

E

E. A. on stamps of Algeria: **Algeria;** on stamps of Greece: **Greece – Aegean Islands – Chio.**

E.A.F. on stamps of Great Britain: **Great Britain – Offices in East Africa – Somalia.**

ΣΑΜΟΥ: Greece – Aegean Islands – Samos.

EAST AFRICA & UGANDA PROTECTORATES with portrait of King George V: if watermarked Multiple Crown and C.A.: **East Africa and Uganda;** of watermarked Multiple Crown and Script C.A.: **Kenya, Uganda, and Tanzania.**

EAST INDIA POSTAGE: India; on stamps with Crown and new denominations: **Straits Settlements.**

EATONTON GEO.: United States – Eatonton, Georgia.

ECUADOR on stamps of Colombia: **Ecuador.**

E.E.F. ("Egyptian Expeditionary Force"): **Palestine.**

EESTI on stamps of Russia: **Estonia.**

EE. UU. DE C.: Colombia – Tolima.

EGEO on stamps of Italy: **Italy – Aegean Islands.**

EGYPTE: Egypt.

EINZUZIEHEN: Danzig – Postage due stamps.

EIRE: Ireland.

EJERCITO RENOVADOR: Mexico – Sonaloa.

EL PARLAMENTO A CERVANTES: Spain – Official stamps.

Elsaß (Alsace) on stamps of Germany: **France – German occupation.**

EL SALVADOR: Salvador.

ELUAKENTA: Hawaii.

EMORY: United States – Emory, Virginia.

EMP. OTTOMAN: Eastern Rumelia, Turkey.

EMPIRE FRANC: France, French Colonies.

ΕΝΑΡΙΘΜΟΝ: **Greece.**

ΕΘΝΙΚΗ: **Greece.**

ЕРМАКБ: South Russia.

EQUATEUR: Ecuador.

E.R. ("Elizabeth Regina") on stamps with queen's head: **Great Britain.**

ESCUELAS: Venezuela.

ESPAÑA SAHARA: Spanish Sahara.

ESPAÑA, ESPAÑOLA: Spain.

ESPAÑS: Spain.

ESTADO DA INDIA: Portuguese India.

ESTADO ESPAÑOL ("Spanish State"): **Spain.**

ESTADOS UNIDOS DE NUEVA GRENADA: Colombia.

EST AFRICAIN ALLEMAND OCCUPATION BELGE on stamps of Congo Democratic Republic (ex-Belgian): **German East Africa.**

ESTERO on stamps of Italy: **Italy – Offices Abroad.**

ÉTABLISSEMENTS DANS L'INDÉ or DE L'INDÉ: French India.

ÉTABLISSEMENTS DE L'OCEANIE: French Polynesia.

ÉTAT DU CAMEROUN: Cameroun.

ÉTAT FRANÇAIS: France.

ETAT IND. DU CONGO ("Independent State of Congo"): **Congo Democratic Republic** (ex-Belgian).

ETIOPIA, ETHIOPIE, ETHIOPIENNES: Ethiopia.

ETS. FRANCS. DE L'OCEANIE: French Polynesia.

E. U. DE COLOMBIA ("United States of Colombia"): **Colombia.**

EUPEN or EUPEN & MALMEDY on stamps of Belgium: **Germany – Belgian occupation.**

EXPED. SCIENT. on stamps with oriental characters: **China.**

EXPOSIÇION DE BARCELONA, EXPOSIÇION GENERAL ESPAÑOLA or EXPOSIÇION GRAL SEVILLA BARCELONA: Spain.

HOW TO COLLECT STAMPS

EXPOSITION COLONIALE INTERNATIONALE PARIS 1931 with no country name: **France.**

EXPOSITION INDUSTRIELLE DAMAS 1929 ("Damascus Industrial Exhibition"): **Syria.**

ΕΛΛΑΣ, ΕΛΛΑΣ ("Hellas") **Greece**; on stamps of Italy: **Italy –**
Ionian Islands – German occupation; on stamps of
Crete: **Crete.**

ΕΛΛΗΝΙΚΗ on stamps of Bulgaria: **Greece – Aegean Islands – Cavilla,**
Dedeagatch, North Epirus, and Occupied Territories.

ΕΛΛΗΝΙΚΗ: **Greece.**

ΕΛΛΗΚΙΚΗ ΔΙΟΚΣΙΣ on stamps of Greece: **Greece – Aegean Islands –**
Icaria.

Ελληυικη Καροχη Μυτιληυησ on stamps of **Greece – Aegean Islands –**
Mytilene.

ΕΛΕΤΟΕΡΑ VONITEIA: **Greece – Aegean Islands – Icaria.**

ΕΔΔ on stamps of Greece: **Greece – Aegean Islands – Dodecanese**
Islands.

F

FACTAJ on stamps of Romania: **Romania** – Parcel post stamps.
FARIDKOT: India – Faridot.
FCFA: Reunion
FDO. POO: Fernando Po.
FEDERATA DEMOKRATIKE MDERKOMETORE: Albania.
FEDERATED MALAY STATES: Malaya.
FEDERATION OF MALAYA: Malaya.
FEDERATION OF MALI: Mali.
FELDPOST on stamps of Germany: **Germany** – Military stamps.
FEN, EN: Manchukuo; FEN on stamps of Poland: **Poland.**
FERANADO POO: Fernanado Po.
FEZZAN or **FEZZAN GHADAMES: Libya** – French occupation.
FIERA DI TRIESTE on stamps of Italy: **Trieste.**
FILIPAS, FILIPINAS: Philippines.
FILLÉR: Hungary.
FILS on stamps with no country name: **Iraq, Jordan.**
FINCASTLE: United States – Fincastle, Virginia.
FIUME on stamps of Hungary: **Fiume.**
FLUCHTINGSHIFE MONTENEGRO on stamps of Jugoslavia: **Montenegro –**
German occupation.
FLUGPOST ("Airmail"): **Austria, Danzig, Germany.**
FORCES FRANCAISE LIBRES-LEVANT: Syria – Free French Administration.

54

fr. on stamps of Sengal: **French West Africa.**

FØROYAR: Faroe Islands

FRANC on stamps of Austria: **Austria – Offices in Crete.**

FRANCA on stamps of Peru: **Peru – Aneanchs, Chicayo.**

FRANÇAISE: France.

FRANCE D'OUTRE-MER: French Colonies.

FRANCO: Philippines, Spain, Switzerland.

FRANCO BOLLO with no country name on perforated stamps: **Italy;**
on imperforated stamps: **Sardinia.**

FRANCOBOLLO DI STATO: Italy – Official stamps.

FRANCO BOLLO POSTALE with denominations in BAJ, SCUDO, CENT.
or CENTESIMI: **Roman States.**

FRANCO SCRISOREI: Romania – Moldavia-Walachia.

FRANK: Austria

FRANKLIN N.C.: United States – Franklin, North Carolina.

FRANQUICIA: Spain.

FREDERICKSB'G: United States – Fredericksburg, Virginia.

FREI DURCH ABLOSUNG ("Free because of prepayment"): **Germany.**

FREIE STADT DANZIG: Danzig.

FREIMARKE with no country name: **Baden, Prussia, Thurn and Taxis,
Wurttemberg.**

FREISTAAT BAYERN on stamps of Germany: **Bavaria.**

FRIMARKE KGL POST: Denmark.

FUNF GROTE: Breman.

FURSTENTTUM or **FVERSTENTUM LIECHTENSTEIN: Liechtenstein.**

G

G or **GW** on stamps of Cape of Good Hope: **Griqualand West.**

GAB. or **GABON** on stamps of French Colonies: **Gabon.**

GALVESTON TEX.: United States – Galveston, Texas.

GARCH: Saudi Arabia.

GARZON: Colombia – Tolima.

G.E.A. on stamps of East Africa and Uganda: **German East Africa –
British occupation**; on stamps of Kenya: **Tankanyika.**

GENERAL GOUVERNEMENT: Poland – German occupation.

GENEVA: Switzerland – Geneva.

GEN – GOUV. WARSCHAU on stamps of Germany: **Poland – German occupation.**

GEORGIE, GEORGIENNE: Georgia.

GEORGETOWN S.C.: United States – Georgetown, South Carolina.

GERUSALEMME on stamps of Italy: **Italy – Offices in Turkey –
Jerusalem.**

GHADAMES: Libya – French occupation.

GHANA on stamps of Gold Coast: **Ghana.**

GIBRALTAR on stamps of Bermuda: **Gibraltar.**

GILBERT & ELLICE PROTECTORATE on stamps of Fiji: **Gilbert and Ellice Islands.**

GIORNALI STAMPE: Sardinia.

GOLFE DE BENIN: Benin.

GOLIAD: United States – Goliad, Texas.

GONZALES TEXAS: United States – Gonzales, Texas.

GOVERNMENT CITY DISPATCH: United States – Baltimore, Maryland.

GOVERNO MILTARE ALLEATO on stamps of Italy: **Italy – Allied occupation.**

GOYA: Spain.

G.P.E. or **G. & D.** on stamps of French Colonies: **Guadeloupe.**

GRAHAMLAND on stamps of Falkland Isalnds: **Falkland Islands – Grahamland.**

GRANA: Two Sicilies.

GRANADINE: Colombia.

GRANDE COMORO: Grand Comoro.

GRAND LIBAN: Lebanon.

GREENSBORO ALA.: United States – Greensboro, Alabama.

GREENSBORO N.C.: United States – Greensboro, North Carolina.

GREENVILLE, ALA.: United States – Greenville, Alabama.

GREENVILLE C.H.S.C.: United States – Greenville Court House, South Carolina.

G.R.I. on stamps inscribed "Deutsch New Guinea": **New Britain;** on stamps of Samoa: **Samoa – German Administration.**

GRIFFIN GA.: United States – Griffin, Georgia.

GRØNLAND: Greenland.

GROSSDEUTSCHES REICH ("Great Germany"): **Germany;** with **BOHMEN UND MAHREN: Czechoslovakia – Bohemia and Moravia.**

GROSSDEUTSCHES REICH GENERALGOVERNEMENT: Poland – German occupation.

GROUCH: Turkey.

GROVE HILL ALA.: United States – Grove Hill, Alabama.

GUADEL: Mexico – Guadel.

GUADELOPE on stamps of French Colonies: **Guadeloupe.**

GUAM on stamps of United States: **Guam.**

GUANACASTE: Costa Rica - Guanacaste.

GUERNSEY: Great Britain – Guernsey.

GUINE or **GUINE PORTUGUESA: Cape Verde, Portuguese Guinea.**

GUINEA followed by **CONTINENTAL, CORREOS,** or **ESPAÑOLA: Spanish Guinea;** by **ECUATORIAL: Equatorial Guinea.**

GUINEE or **GUINEE FRANÇAIS:** French Guinea.

GULTIG 9 ARMEE on stamps of Germany: Romania – German occupation.

GUYANA on stamps of British Guiana: Guyana.

GUYANE FRANÇAISE: French Guiana.

GUY. FRANC. on stamps of France: French Guiana.

GWALIOR: India – Gwalior.

G. Л. О. ONZ on stamps of Russia: Russia – Offices in Turkey.

H

HABILADO in stamps of Cuba: Cuba – U.S. Administration.

HALLETTSVILLE TEX: United States – Hallettsville, Texas.

HAMBURG S.C.: United States – Hamburg, South Carolina.

HASHEMITE KINGDOM OF JORDAN: Jordan.

HATAY DEVLETI: Hatay.

HAUTE SILESIE: Upper Silesia.

HAUTE VOLTA: Upper Volta.

HAUT-SENEGAL-NIGER: Upper Senegal and Niger.

H.E.H. THE NIZAN'S: India – Hyderabad.

HEJAZ & NEJD, HEDJAZ & NEDJDE: Saudi Arabia.

HELENA: United States – Helena, Texas.

HELLER: Austria, Bosnia-Herzegovina, Liechtenstein.

HELVETIA: Switzerland.

H.H. NAWAB SHAH JAHANBECAM: India – Bhopal.

H.I. or **HAWAIIAN ISLANDS POSTAGE:** Hawaii.

H.I. & U.S.: Hawaii.

HIRLAPJEGY: Hungary.

НОВЧ, НОВЧИЧ: Montenegro.

HOI HAO on stamps of Indo-China: France – Offices in China –
          Hoi Hao.

HOLKAR STATE: India – Indore.

HOLSTEIN: Schleswig-Holstein.

HONDOUR'S: United States – Charlestown, South Carolina.

HOUSTON TXS: United States – Houston, Texas.

Н. Р. БЪАГАРИЯ: Bulgaria.

HRVATSKA: Croatia, Jugoslavia.

HRZGL.: Schleswig-Holstein.

HT SENEGAL-NIGER: Upper Senegal and Niger.

HUNGARIC REPUBLICA: Hungary.

HUNTSVILLE TEX.: United States – Huntsville, Texas.

HYDERABAD: India – Hyderabad.

ΗΓΙΕΙΡΟΣ: Epirus.

I

ICC on stamps of India: **India – International Commission in Indo-China – Laos and Vietnam.**

IDAR: India – Idar.

I.E.F. ("Indian Expeditionary Force"): **India.**

I.E.F.'D' on stamps of Turkey: **Mesopotamia.**

IERUSALM on stamps of Russia: **Russia – Offices in Turkey.**

ILE DE LA RÉUNION: Reunion.

ILE ROUAD on stamps of French offices in the Levant: **Rouad.**

ILES WALLIS ET FUTUNA: Wallis and Futuna Islands.

IMPERIAL BRITISH EAST AFRICA COMPANY: British East Africa.

IMPERIAL CHINESE POST, CHINESE IMPERIAL POST or CHINESE EMPIRE: China.

IMPERIAL JAPANESE POST: Japan.

IMPERIAL KOREAN POST: Korea.

IMPERIO COLONIAL PORTUGUES with no colony name: **Portuguese Africa.**

IMPTO or IMPUESTO DE GUERRA: Spain.

INCI YIL DONUMU: Turkey.

INDE, INDIE: French India.

INDEPENDENCE, TEX.: United States – Independence, Texas.

INDIA with inscriptions in Portuguese or words REIS, TANGAS, or RUPIA: **Portuguese India.**

INDIA PORT. or PORTUGUEZA: Portuguese India.

INDO CHINE: Indo-China.

INDONESIA not preceded by "REPUBIK": **Dutch Indies – Indonesia.**

INDORE: India – Indore.

INDUSTRIELLE KRIEGSWIRTSCHAFT: Switzerland.

INHAMBANE on stamps of Mozambique: **Inhambane.**

INKERI: North Ingermanland.

INLAND: Liberia.

INSELPOST on stamps of Germany: **Germany** – military stamps.

INSTRUCAO on stamps of Portuguese India: **Timor.**

INSTRUCCION: Venezuela.

INSUFFICIENTLY PREPAID POSTAGE DUE: Zanzibar.

IONIKAPATOΣ: Ionian Islands.

I. O. V. R.: Romania.

IRAN: Persia.

IRANIENNES ("Iranien"): **Persia.**

IRAQ on stamps of Turkey: **Mesopotamia.**

IRIAN BARAT: West New Guinea.

I.R. OFFICIAL on stamps of Great Britain: **Great Britain –** Official stamps.

ISLAND: Iceland.

ISLAS GALAPAGOS: Ecuador – Galapagos Islands.

ISLE OF MAN: Great Britain – Man, Isle of.

ISOLE ITALIANE DELL'EGEO on stamps of Italy: **Italy – Aegean Islands.**

ISOLE JONIE on stamps of Italy: **Ionian Islands – Italian occupation.**

ISTRA or **ISTRIA: Jugoslavia – Issues for Istria and the Slovene Coast.**

ΙΤΑΑΙΑΣ-ΕΛΛΑΔΟΣ-ΤΟΥΡΚΙΑ: **Greece.**

ITA-KARJALA on stamps inscribed "SUOMI-FINLAND": **Karelia –** Finnish administration.

ITALIA, ITALINE, ITALIANO: Italy.

ITALIAN SOMALILAND: Somalia.

ITALIA OCCUPAZONE MILITARE ITALIANA ISOLE CAFALONIA E ITACA on stamps of Greece: **Ionian Islands – Italian occupation.**

I-U-KA: United States – Inka, Mississippi.

IZMIR HIMAYEIETFAL: Turkey.

J

JAFFA on stamps of Russia: **Russia – Offices in Turkey.**

JAIPUR: India – Jaipur.

JAMES M BUCHANAN: United States – Baltimore, Maryland.

JAMHURIZANZIBAR TANZANIA: Zanzibar.

JANINA on stamps of Italy: **Italy – Offices in Turkey – Janina.**

JAPANESE EMPIRE: Japan.

JAVA on stamps inscribed "Nederlandsch-Indie": **Dutch Indies.**

JEEND STATE: India – Jhind.

JERSEY: Great Britain – Jersey.

JERUSALEM on stamps of Russia: **Russia – Offices in Turkey.**

JIND, JHIND: India – Jhind.

JOHORE, JOHOR: Malay States – Johore.

JONESBORO T.: United States – Jonesboro, Tennessee.

JOURNAUX DAGBLADEN on stamps of Belgium: **Belgium –** Newspaper stamps.

J. P. JOHNSON, P. M.: United States – Pittsylvania Court House, Virginia.

JUBILE DE L'UNION POSTALE UNIVERSELLE: Switzerland.

ЈУГОСЛАВИЈА: **Jugoslavia.**

K

K with no country name (abbreviation for Krone): **Bosnia and** Herzegovina.

KAISKON: Austria.

KALAYAAN NANG PLIPINAS: Philippines – Japanese occupation.

KALIPEDIA: Memel – Lithuanian occupation.

KAMERUN: Cameroun.

KAP: Latvia.

КАРПАТСЬКА-УКРАІНА on stamps inscribed "Cesko-Slovensko":
          Czechoslovakia – Carpath-Ukraine.

KARJALA: Karelia.

KARKI on stamps of Italy: Italy – Aegean Islands – Karki.

KARLFONDS: Austria, Bosnia & Herzegovina.

KÄRNTEN ABSTIMMUNG ("Carinthian Plebisite") on stamps of Austria:
          Austria.

KAROLINEN: Caroline Islands.

К. С. ПОУТА or **КСГБСКА:** Serbia.

KEDAH: Malay States – Kedah.

KELANTAN: Malay States – Kelantan.

KEMAHKOTAAN or **KETAHKOTAAN** on stamps inscribed "Johore": Malay
          States – Johore.

KENTTA-POSTI or **KENTTA-POSTIA:** Finland – Military stamps.

KENYA & UGANDA: Kenya, Uganda and Tanzania.

KENYA UGANDA TANGANYIKA: Kenya, Uganda, and Tanzania.

KERASSUNDE on stamps of Russia: Russia – Offices in Turkey.

K. G. L. or **KONGELIGT:** Danish West Indes, Denmark.

KHMER REPUBLIC: Cambodia.

KHOR FAKKAN: Sharjah and Dependencies.

KIAUTSCHOU: Kiauchau.

KIBRIS CUMHURIYETI: Cyprus.

KINGSTON GA.: United States – Kingston, Georgia.

KIONGA on stamps or Lourenço Marques: Kionga.

KISHANGARH: India – Kishengarh.

K.K. or **KAISERLICHE KONIGLICHE OSTERREICHISCHE POST** ("Imperial
          and Royal Austrian Post"): Austria.

KK-POST-STEMPEL with values in **KREUZER:** Austria; with values in
          CENTES: Austria – Lombardy–Venetia.

K-numeral-K on stamps of Russia: Far Eastern Republic.

K 60 K on stamps of Russia: Armenia.

KNOXVILLE: United States – Knoxville, Tennessee.

КОН, КОП, KON: Batum, Far Eastern Republic, Finland, Latvia,
          Russia, South Russia.

KOP: Finland.

KORCA or **KORCE:** Albania.

KOREAN POST: Korea.

KORONA: Hungary.

KOUANG-TCHEOU or **KOUANGTCHEOUWAN** on stamps of Indo-China:
　　　France – **Offices in China** – **Kwangchowan.**

КРАЈЬЕВСТВО C.X.C.: Jugoslavia.

KPALJEVSTVO or **KRALJEVINA SRBA, HRVATA I SLOVENACA** ("Kingdom
　　　of the Serbs, Croats and Slovenes"): **Jugoslavia.**

КРНТН: Crete.

KR., KREUZER: Austria, Baden, Bavaria, Germany, Hungary, Wurttemburg.

KRAIЬ. УВНАГОРА: Montenegro.

KRONE, KRONEN: Austria.

K.S.A.: (Kingdom of) Saudi Arabia

K.U.K. ("Imperial and Royal"): **Austria, Bosnia and Herzegovina.**

K-U-K-FELDPOST: Austria; with values in "BANI" or "LEI": **Romania.**

K-U-K-MILITARPOST: Bosnia and Herzegovina.

K. UND K. FELDPOST: Austria.

KUWAIT on stamps of India or Great Britain: **Kuwait.**

K. WURTT: Wurttemburg.

КИТАИ on stamps of Russia: **Russia – Offices in China.**

L

LA AGUERA: Aguera.

LABUAN on stamps of North Borneo: **Labuan.**

LA CANEA on stamps of Italy: **Italy – Offices in Crete.**

LA GEORGIE: Georgia.

LA GRANGE TEX.: United States – LaGrange, Texas.

LAIBACH: Jugoslavia – Ljubijana – German occupation.

LAKE CITY FLA.: United States – Lake City, Florida.

LANSA: Colombia.

L.A.R. (Libyan Arab Republic): **Libya.**

LAS BELA: India – Las Bela.

LATTAQUIE on stamps of Syria: **Latakia.**

LATVIJA, LATWIJA: Latvia.

LAVACA: United States – Port Lavaca, Texas.

LAVANTE on stamps of Italy: **Italy – Offices in Turkey.**

LEI on stamps of Austria: **Romania – Austrian occupation.**

LENIOR N.C.: United States – Lenoir, North Carolina.

LEROS or **LERO** on stamps of Italy: **Italy – Aegean Islands – Leros.**

LESTHO on stamps of Basutoland: **Lestho.**

LEVA: Bulgaria.

LEVANT: France – Offices in Turkey; on stamps of Great Britain:
　　　Great Britain – Offices in Turkey; on stamps of Poland:
　　　Poland – Offices in Turkey.

LEXINGTON, MISS: United States – Lexington, Mississippi.

LIBAN, LIBANAISE: Lebanon.

LIBAU on stamps of Germany: **Latvia – German occupation.**

LIBIA, LIBYE: Libya; on stamps of Cyrenaica: **Libya.**

LIETUVA, LIETVOS: Lithuania; on stamps of Russia: **Lithuania – South District.**

LIGNES AERIENNE F.A.F.L. or **LIGNES AERIENNE DE LA FRANCE LIBRE: Syria – Free French Administration.**

LIMA: Peru.

LIMBAGAN – 1543-1943 on stamps of Philippines: **Philippines – Japanese occupation.**

LIPSO, LISSO on stamps of Italy: **Italy – Aegean Islands – Lisso.**

LIRE on stamps of Austria: **Italy – Austrian occupation.**

LISBOA: Portugal.

LITAS: Lithuania.

LITWA SRODKOWA, LITWY SRODKOWEI: Central Lithuania.

LIVINGSTON: United States – Livingston, Alabama.

LJUBLJANSKA: Jugoslavia – Ljubljana – German occupation.

L. MARQUES on stamps of Mozambique: **Louenço Marques.**

LOCKPORT N.Y.: United States – Lockport, New York.

LÖSEN: Sweden.

LOTHRIGEN on stamps of Germany: **France – German occupation.**

L. P. on stamps of Russia: **Latvia.**

LTSR on stamps of Lithuania: **Lithuania – Russian occupation.**

LUBIANA on stamps of Jugoslavia: **Jugoslavia – Ljubljana – Italian occupation.**

LUFTELDPOST: Germany – Military air post stamps.

LUXEMBURG: Luxembourg; on stamps of Germany: **Luxembourg – German occupation.**

M

MACAU or **MACAV: Macao.**

MACON: United States – Macon, Georgia.

MADIERA on stamps of Portugal: **Maderia.**

MADRID: Spain.

MAGYAR ("Hungarian"): **Hungary.**

MAGYAR KIR.: Hungary.

MAGARKIRALY or **MAGY. KIR: Hungary.**

MAGYAR NEMZEMI KORMANY SZEGED on stamps of Hungary: **Hungary – Serbian occupation – Szeged.**

MAGYARORZÁG: Hungary.

MALACCA: Malay States – Malacca.

MALAGA on stamps of Spain: **Spain – Malaga.**

MALAGASY: Madagascar.

MALAYA with no further inscriptions, over portrait of Sultan:
Malaya States – Kelantan, Negri Sembilan, Pahang, Perak, Perlis, Selangor, Trengganu; over picture of mosque: **Selangor**; over picture of state arms: **Negri Sembilan.**

MALGACHE: Madagascar.

MALDIVES: Maldive Islands.

MALMEDY on stamps of Belgium: **Germany – Belgian occupation.**

MANAMA: a dependency of Ajman.

MAPKA: Finland, Russia, Serbia.

MARCA DA BOLLO: Italy.

MARIAM: Mariana Islands.

MARIANS ESPAÑOLAS on stamps inscribed "Filpnas": **Mariana Islands – Spanish Dominion.**

MARIETTA: United States – Marietta, Georgia.

MARION VA.: United States – Marion, Virginia.

MARK, MARKKAA: Finland.

MARKA: Estonia.

MAROC: French Morocco, Morocco.

MAROCCO, MAROKKO on stamps of Germany: **Germany – Offices in Morocco.**

MARREUCOS: Morocco – Northern Zone, Spanish Morocco.

MARSHALL-INSELN: Marshall Islands.

MARTINIQUE on stamps of French Colonies: **Martinique.**

MAURITANIE: Mauritania.

M.B.D. on stamps inscribed "Raj Nandoan": **India – Nandgoan.**

MBLEDHJA on stamps of Albania: **Albania – Italian dominion.**

MBRENTNIJA SHQUPTARE, MBLEDHJEA KUSTETUE, MBR. SHIQTAR, MBRETNIA SHGYPTARE: Albania.

M.C. GALLAWA: United States – Memphis, Tennessee.

MECKLEMB. SCHERIN: Mecklenburg-Schwerin.

MEDELLIN: Colombia, Colombia – Antioqua.

MEDIA ONZA: Spain.

MEDIO REAL: Dominican Republic.

M.E.F. on stamps of Great Britain: **Great Britain – Offices in Africa.**

MEJICO: Mexico.

MELAKA: Malay States – Malacca.

MEMELGEBIET ("Memal Territory"): Memal.

MEMPHIS TENN.: United States – Memphis, Tennessee.

METELIN on stamps of Russia: **Russia – Offices in Turkey.**

MEXICANO ("Mexican"): **Mexico.**

MICANOPY FLA.: United States – **Micanopy, Florida.**

MILIT or **MILITARPOST PORTOMARKE** or **ELLMARKE: Bosnia and Herzegovina.**

MILL., MILLIEMES on stamps of France: **France** – **Offices in Egypt.**

MILLEDGEVILLE GA.: United States – **Milledgeville, Georgia.**

M. KIR. ("Magyar Kirly"): **Hungary.**

MN: Korea.

MOBILE, ALA.: United States – **Mobile, Alabama.**

MOÇAMBIQUE: Mozambique.

MONGTZE, MONGTSEU on stamps of Indo-China: **France** – **Offices in China** – **Mongtseu.**

MONROVIA: Liberia.

MONT ATHOS on stamps of Russia: **Russia** – **Offices in Turkey.**

MONTENEGRO on stamps of Austria: **Montenegro** – **Austrian occupation;** on stamps of Jugoslavia: **Montenegro** – **Italian occupation.**

MONTEVIDEO: Uruguay.

MONTGOMERY: United States – **Montgomery, Alabama.**

MONTSERRAT on stamps of Antigua: **Montserrat.**

MOQUEGRA, MOQUEA on stamps inscribed "Peru" or "Franqued": **Peru** – **Moquegua.**

MOΓA: Ukrain.

MOROCCO AGENCIES on stamps of Great Britain: **Great Britain** – **Offices in Morocco.**

MORVI: India – **Morvi.**

MOYEN CONGO: Middle Congo.

MQE on stamps of French Colonies: **Martinique.**

MULTA: Portugal and Portuguese Colonies – Postage due stamps.

MUSCAT & OMAN: Oman.

M.V.I.R. on stamps of Germany or Romania: **Romania** – **German occupation.**

N

NABAH: India – **Nabah.**

NACIONES UNIDAS: United Nations.

NANADGAON: India – **Nandigaon.**

ΠAPA: Serbia.

NAPOLETANA: Two Sicilies.

NASHVILLE: United States – **Nashville, Tennessee.**

NA SLASK: Central Lithuania.

NATIONALER VERWAILTUGSAUSSCHUSS on stamps of Montenegro: **Montenegro** – **German occupation.**

NATIONS UNIES: United Nations.

NAURU on stamps of Great Britain: **Nauru.**

N.C.E. on stamps of French Colonies: **New Caledonia.**

N. D. HRVATSKA: Croatia.

ΛΕΒΑ, ΛΕΒЬ: Bulgaria.

NEDERLAND: Netherlands.

NED-INDIE, NEDERL-INDIE, NEDERLANDSCH-INDIE: Dutch Indies.

NED or NEDERLANDSE ANTILLEN: Netherlands Antillies.

NED or NEDERLANDS NIEUW GUINEA: Dutch New Guinea.

NEGERI SEMBILAN: Malay States – Negri Sembilan.

NEW HAVEN CT.: United States – New Haven, Connecticut.

NEW HEBRIDES CONDOMINUM on stamps of Fiji: **New Hebrides.**

NEW ORLEANS or **N.O.P.O.: United States – New Orleans, Louisiana.**

NEW YORK: United States – New York, New York.

NEZAVISNA DRZAVA HRVATSKA: Croatia.

NEZ. DRZ. HRVATSKA: Croatia.

N.F. on stamps of Nyasaland Protectorate: **German East Africa –
      British occupation.**

NIEUW GUINEA: Dutch New Guinea.

NIEUW REPUBLIK: New Republic.

NIPPON: Japan.

NISIROS or **NISIRO** on stamps of Italy: **Italy – Aegean Islands –
      Nisiro.**

NIUE on stamps of New Zealand: **Niue.**

NILLE CALEDONIE: New Caledonia.

NO HAY ESTAMPILLES: Colombia – many states.

ПОРТО МАРКА ("postage due"): **Serbia.**

NORDDEUTSCHER POST-BEZIRK ("North German Postal District"):

      Germany – North German Confederation.

NOREG: Norway.

NORFOLK ISLAND on stamps of Australia: **Norfolk Island.**

NORGE: Norway.

NOSSI-BE on stamps of French Colonies: **Nossi-Be.**

NOUVELLE CALEDONIE: New Caledonia.

NOUVELLES HEBRIDES: New Hebrides (French Issues)

ПОЩАВЪ РОПЖИИЯ: Romania – Bulgarian occupation.

NOWANUGGUR: India – Nowanuggur.

ПОЩТА: Serbia.

ПОЧТА ("postage"): **Russia.**

ПОЧТ МАРКА on stamps with no country name: **Azerbaijan.**

ПОЧТОВАЯ МАРКА: Finland.

ΠΡΟΣΩΡΙΝΟΝ or **ΠΡΟΕΩΡΤΑΧΤΔΡ: Crete.**

N.S.B. on stamps of French Colonies: **Nossi-Be.**

N. SEMBILAN: Malay States – Negri Sembilan.

N.S.W.: New South Wales.

N.W. PACIFIC ISLANDS on stamps of Australia: North West Pacific Islands.

NYASALAND: Nyasaland Protectorate.

NYASSA on stamps of Mozambique: Nyassa.

N.Z.: New Zealand.

O

ОДНА МАКА: Finland.

OAXACA: Mexico – Oaxaco.

OBOCK on stamps of French Colonies: Obock.

OCCUPATION FRANCAISE on stamps of Hungary: Hungary – French occupation.

OCEANIE: French Polynesia.

OESTERR POST: Austria; with name Liechtenstein: Liechtenstein – Austrian postal administration.

OEUVRES DE SOLIDARITE FRANCAISE: French Colonies.

OFFENTIG SAK: Norway.

OFFICIAL on stamps of Kenya, Uganda and Tanzania: Tanganika.

OFFISIEEL ("Official"): South Africa, South West Africa.

OFF. SAK.: Norway – Official stamps.

ÖFTERREICH: Austria.

OIL RIVERS: Niger Coast Protectorate.

OKCA: Russia – Army of the North.

OLTRE GIUBA on stamps of Italy: Oltre Giumba.

O.M.F. SYRIE on stamps of France: Syria.

ORANGE RIVER COLONY on stamps of Cape of Good Hope: Orange River Colony.

ORANJE VRIJ STAAT ("Orange Free State"): Orange River Colony.

ORCHA: India – Orcha.

ÖRE: Danmark, Norway, Sweden.

ÖRTS-POST: Switzerland.

O.S.: Norway.

ÖSTERREICH: Austria.

OSTERR-POST, OSTERREICHISCHE POST: Austria.

OSTLAND ("Eastland") on stamps of Germany: Russia – German occupation.

OTVORENIE SLOVENSKENO on stamps of Czechoslovakia: Czechoslovakia – Slovakia.

OUBANGUI-CHARI: Ubangi.

O. W. OFFICIAL on stamps of Great Britain: Great Britain – Official stamps.

ΟΛΥΜ., ΟΛΥΜΠΙΑΚΟΙ ("Olympic"): Greece.
ΟΔΥΜΠ: *Greece.*

P

P on stamps of Straits Settlements: **Malay States – Perak.**

p (pence) or £ (pound) preceded by a numeral, on stamps with
kings or queen's head but no country name: **Great
Britain.**

PACCI POSTALI ("Parcel Post"): Italy; with value in diagonal
band: **Sam Marino;** with star and crescent emblem:
Somalia.

PACKHOI or PAK-HOI on stamps of Indo-China: **France–Offices in
China – Packhoi.**

PAHANG: **Malay States – Pahang.**

PAID with value in cents: **United States** – various provisionals.

PAIS, PICE: **Nepal.**

PAITA on stamps of Peru: **Peru – Paita.**

PAKISTAN on stamps of India: **Pakistan.**

PAKKE-PORTO: **Greenland.**

PALESTINE on stamps of Egypt: **Egypt – Palestine occupation.**

PAPUA on stamps of British New Guinea: **Papua New Guinea.**

PAPUA & NEW GUINEA: **Papua New Guinea.**

PARA or PARAS: Egypt, Mesopotamia, Turkey; on stamps of Austria:
Austria – Offices in Turkey; on stamps of Germany:
Germany – Offices in Turkey; on stamps of Great Britain:
Great Britain – Offices in Turkey; on stamps of
Romania: **Romania – Offices in Turkey;** on stamps
of Russia: **Russia – Offices in Turkey;** on stamps
of France: **France – Offices on Turkey;** on stamps of
Italy: **Italy – Offices in Turkey.**

PASCO on stamps of Peru: **Peru – Pasco.**

PATIALA: **India – Patiala.**

PATMOS or PATMO on stamps of Italy: **Italy – Aegean Islands –
Patmo.**

P.C.Φ.C.P. (abbreviation for "Russian Soviet Socialist Republic"):
Russia.

P.E. inscribed on stamps with arabic overprints: **Egypt.**

PECHINO on stamps of Italy: **Italy – Offices in China – Peking.**

PEN, PENNI, PENNIAS: Finland.

PENNY: **United States** – various provisionals.

PENRHYN ISLAND on stamps of Cook Islands or New Zealand: **Penrhyn Island.**

PEOPLE'S DEMOCRATIC REPUBLIC OF YEMEN: Yemen, People's Democratic Republic.

PEOPLE'S REPUBLIC OF SOUTHERN YEMEN: on stamps of South Arabia: Yemen, People's Democratic Republic.

PERAK: Malay States – Perak.

PERLIS: Malay States – Perlis.

PERSANE: Persia.

PERSEKUTAN TANAH MELAYU: Malaya.

PERUANA: Peru.

PERV-AERO: Peru – air post.

PESA on stamps of Germany: **German East Africa.**

PESETAS with no country name: **Spain.**

PETERSBURG VIRGINIA: United States – Petersburg, Virginia.

PF or **PFG** on stamps of Germany: **Germany – Officies in China, Kaiauchau;** on stamps of Russia: **Estonia – German occupation.**

PFENNIG: Barvaria, Germany, Wuttemberg.

P.G.S. on stamps of Straits Settlements: **Malay States – Perak.**

PHILIPPINE ISLANDS: Philippines.

PHILIPPINES on stamps of United States: **Philippines – U.S. Administration.**

PIASTER: Austria – Officies in Turkey; Germany – Officies in Turkey.

PIASTRA, PIASTRE, PIASTRES on stamps of Italy: **Italy – Officies in Crete** or in Turkey; on stamps of Italy: **Italy – Officies Great Britain – Officies in Turkey;** on stamps of Russia: **Russia – Officies in Turkey;** on stamps of France: **France – Officies in Turkey.**

PIASTRO on stamps of Italy: **Italy – Officies in Crete.**

PIES: India.

PILGRIM TECENTENARY with no country name: **United States.**

PILIPINAS: Philippines.

PINSIN: Ireland.

PISCO on stamps of Peru: **Peru – Pisco.**

PISCOPI on stamps of Italy: **Italy – Aegean Islands – Piscopi.**

PIURA on stamps of Peru: **Peru – Piura.**

PLEASENT SHADE: United States – Pleasent Shade, Virginia.

PLEBISCITE OLSZTYN ALLENSTEIN on stamps of Germany: **Allenstein.**

PLEBISCIT SLESVIG: Schleswig.

P.M. on stamps of Italy: **Italy** – Military stamps.

POCCИЯ: Russia, South Russia.

POCZTA: Poland.

POCZTA POLSKA ("Polish postage"): **Poland**; on stamps of Germany:
Germany – Polish occupation; on stamps of Austria:
Poland; on stamps inscribed "Waszara": **Poland.**

POHJOIS INKERI: North Ingermanland.

POLSKA: Poland.

POLYNESIE FRANCAISE: French Polynesia.

PONCE, P.R.: Puerto Rico – Ponce.

Р.О.П.И.Т. on stamps of Russia: **Russia – Offices in Turkey,**
Ukrain.

PORTEADO: Portugal.

PORTE DE CONDUCCION: Peru.

PORTE DE MAR: Mexico.

PORTE FRANCO: Peru, Portugal.

PORT GDANSK on stamps of Poland: **Poland – Offices in Danzig.**

PORT LAGOS on stamps of French colonies: **France – Offices in**
Turkey – Port Lagos.

PORTO on stamps with no country name: **Austria**; with "piastre":
Austria – Offices in Turkey.

PORTO GAZETEI: Romania – Moldavia.

PORTOMARK: Bosnia & Herzegovina.

PORTO RICO on stamps of United States: **Puerto Rico.**

PORT-SAID: France – Offices in Egypt – Port Said.

POŠTA ČESKOSLOVENSKA on stamps of Austria: **Czechoslovakia.**

POSTAGE with value in pies, annas or rupees: **India – Hyderabad**;
with **CAMB. AUST. CIGILLUM NOV** in a circle: **New South Wales.**

POSTAGE, POSTAGE & REVENUE with denominations in d or p (pence)
/ (shilling) or £ (pound) and portraits of a king
or queen, but no country name: **Great Britain**; with
denominations in annas: **India – Kishergarh.**

POSTAGE I.E.F.'D' on stamps of Turkey: **Mesopotamia.**

POSTAGE DUE with denominations in d or p (pence), / (shilling).
or £ (pound): **Australia, Great Britain.**

POSTAGE TWO CENTS with portrait of Andrew Jackson, and initials
C.S. in lower corners: **United States – Confederate**
States.

POSTALI: Italy; with value in diagonal band: **San Marino**; with
star and crescent emblem: **Somalia.**

POSTA ROMANA CONSTANTINOPOL on stamps of Romania: **Romania –**
Offices in Turkey.

POSTAS LE NIOC or **N'LOC: Ireland.**

POSTE AERIEO or **POSTE AERIENNE** on stamps with no country name:
Persia.

POSTE followed by **EGYPTIENES:** Egypt; followed by **HEDJAZ AND NEJDE:** Saudi Arabia; followed by **OTTOMANES:** Mesopotamia, Turkey; followed by picture of crescent: **Afghanistan.**

POSTE CENTIME with numeral in center of stamp, covered with a network of colored lines: **France – Alsace and Lorraine – German occupation.**

POSTE ESTENSI: Modena.

POSTEK NEDEUIERGIZIAHNE or **POSIEXHEDEVIEECIZANE: Egypt.**

POSTE LOCAL: Switzerland – various cantons.

POSTES: Belgium, France, French Colonies, Luxembourg.

POSTES PERSANES: Bushire, Persia.

POSTE VATICANE: Vatican City.

POSTGEBIET OB. OFT on stamps of Germany: **Lithuania – German occupation.**

POST OFFICE DISPATCH: United States – Baltimore, Maryland.

POST STAMP, POST & RECEIPT with values on annas: **India – Hyderabad.**

POSTZEGEL with no country name: **Netherlands.**

POUL: Afghanistan.

PREUSSEN: Prussia.

PRINCE FAROUK: Egypt.

PRINCIPAUTE DE MONCO ("Principality of Monaco"): **Monaco.**

PRO TACNA Y ARICA, PLEBISCITO TACNAYRICA: Peru.

PROJECT MERCURY: United States.

PROTECTORADO ESPAÑOL or with **EN MARRUECOS** on stamps of Spain: **Spanish Morocco.**

PROTECORATES on stamps of Becuanaland: **Becuanaland Protectorate.**

PROTECTORAT FRANCAIS on stamps inscribed "Chiffre Taxe": **French Morocco.**

PRO TUBERCULOSOS POBRES: Spain.

PRO UNION IBEROAMERICANA ("For the Spanish American Union"): **Spain.**

PROVINCIE MODONES: Modena.

PROVINZ LAIBACH: Jugoslavia – Ljubljana – German occupation.

PROVISIONAL 1881-1882 on stamps inscribed "Peru" or "Franqued": **Peru – Arequipa.**

PROV. R.I.: United States – Providence, Rhode Island.

PS: Colombia – Cauca.

P.S.N.C. letters on four corners: **Peru.**

PTO. RICO, PUERTO RICO: Puerto Rico.

PUL: Afghanistan.

PUNO on stamps inscribed "Peru" or "Franqued": **Peru – Puno.**

PUTTIALA on stamps of India: **India – Patiala.**

РУВ or **РУЬ: Finland, Russia, Siberia, South Russia.**

РУССКАЯ ПОУТА, РУССОИ АРМИН on stamps of Russia or Ukrain: **Russia – Offices in Turkey – Wrangel Issues.**

Q

QATAR on stamps of Great Britain: **Qatar.**

QARKU: **Albania.**

QINDAR, QINTAR: **Albania.**

QUELIMANE on stamps of various Portuguese Colonies: **Quelimane.**

R

R on stamp covered with Arabic writing: **India – Jhind.**

R on stamps of Colombia: **Panama.**

R (for "rial") on stamp with Arabic lettering, but no country name: **Persia.**

RAJASTHAN on stamps of Jaipur: **India – Rajasthan.**

RALEIGH N.C.: **United States – Raleigh, North Carolina.**

RAPPEN: **Switzerland.**

RARATONGA on stamps of New Zealand: **Cook Islands.**

RAU on stamps of Syria: **Syria – United Arab Republic.**

RAYON: **Switzerland.**

RECARGO: **Spain.**

RECUEROD DEL I'DE FEBRERO: **Honduras.**

REGATUL ROMANIEI ("Roumanian Kingdom") on stamps of Hungary: **Hungary – Roumanian occupation.**

REGENCE DE TUNIS: **Tunisia.**

REGNO D'ITALIA ("Kingdom of Italy"): **Italy**; on stamps of Austria with words VENEZIA GIULIA or with TRENTINO: **Austria – Italian occupation**; on stamps inscribed FIVME or FIUME: **Fiume.**

REICH, REICHSPOST; **Germany.**

REIS with no country name: **Portugal.**

REP. DI S. MARINO: **San Marino.**

REPOBIKA MALAGASY: **Madagascar.**

REPUBBLICA ITALIANA: **Italy.**

REPUBBLICA SOCIALE ITALIANA: **Italy – Italian Socialist Republic.**

REPUBLICA DE COLOMBIA: **Colombia, Panama.**

REPUBLICA DOMINICANA: **Dominican Republic.**

REPUBLICA ESPAÑOLA: **Spain.**

REPUBLICA ORIENTAL ("Eastern Republic"): **Uruguay.**

REPUBLICA PERUANA: **Peru.**

REPUBLICA POPULARA ROMANIA: Romania.

REPUBLICA PORTUGUESA: Portugal.

REPUBLICA QUELIMANE on stamps of various Portuguese Colonies:
Quelimane.

REPUBLICA TETE on stamps of various Portuguese Colonies: Tete.

REPUBLIC OF BOTSWANA on stamps of Bechuanaland Protectorate:
Botswana.

REPUBLIEK VAN SUID-AFRIKA: South Africa.

REPUBLIKA NG. PILINAS: Philippines – Japanese occupation.

REPUBLIKA POPULLORE E SHQIPERISE: Albania.

REPUBLIK INDONESIA: Indonesia.

REPUBLIQUE ARABE SYRIENNE: Syria.

REPUBLIQUE ARABE UNIE: Syria – United Arab Republic.

REPUBLIQUE AUTONOME DU TOGO: Togo.

REPUBLIQUE CENTRAFRICANE: Central African Republic.

REPUBLIQUE d'AZERBAIJAN: Azerbaijan.

REPUBLIQUE DE COTE D'IVORE: Ivory Coast.

REPUBLIQUE DE GUINEE: Guinea.

REPUBLIQUE DE HAUTE VOLTA: Upper Volta.

REPUBLIQUE DEMOCRATIQUE DU CONGO: Congo Democratic Republic
(ex-Belgian).

REPUBLIQUE D'HAITI: Haiti.

REPUBLIQUE DU CONGO: Congo Democratic Republic (ex-Belgian),
Congo People's Republic (ex-French).

REPUBLIQUE DU DAHOMY: Dahomy.

REPUBLIQUE DU MALI: Mali.

REPUBLIQUE DU NIGER: Niger.

REPUBLIQUE DU SENEGAL: Senegal.
name: France, French Colonies.

REPUBLIQUE DU TCHAD: Chad.

REPUBLIQUE DU TOGO: Togo.

REPUBLIQUE DU ZAIRE: Congo Democratic Republic (ex-Belgian).

REPUB. FRANC. or REPUBLIQUE FRANÇAISE if perforated: France;
if imperforated: French Colonies.

REPUBLIQUE GABONAISE: Gabon.

REPUBLIQUE ISLAMIQUE DE MAURITANIE: Mauritania.

REPUBLIQUE LIBANAISE: Lebanon.

REPUBLIQUE MALGACHE: Madagascar.

REPUBLIQUE POPULAIRE DU CONGO: Congo People's Republic (ex-French)

REPUBLIQUE RWANDAISE: Rwanda.

REPUBLIQUE TOGOLAISE: Togo.

REPUBLIQUE TUNISIENNE: Tunisia.

HOW TO COLLECT STAMPS

RETYMNO: Crete.

REUNION on stamps of French Colonies: **Reunion.**

R. COMMISSARIATO, etc. on stamps of Jugoslavia: **Jugoslavia –
  Ljubljana – Italian occupation.**

R.F. (Abbreviation for "Republic of France") with no country

R.H. (Abbreviation for "Republic of Haiti"): **Haiti.**

RHEATOWN: United States – Rheatown, Tennessee.

RHEINLAND-PFALZ: Germany – Rhine Palatinate – French occupation.

RIAL or **RIALS: Persia.**

RIALTAR SEALDAC NA HEIREANN ("Provisional Government of Ireland")
  on stamps of Great Britain: **Ireland.**

RIAU on stamps of Indonesia: **Indonesia – Riouw Archipelago.**

RICHMOND TEXAS: United States – Richmond, Texas.

RIGGOLD GEORGIA: United States – Riggold, Georgia.

RIN, RN.: Japan.

RIO DE ORO on stamps inscribed "TERRITORIOS ESPANDLES DEL
  AFRICA OCCIDENTAL": **Rio De Oro.**

RIS on stamps of Dutch Indies: **Indonesia.**

RIZEH on stamps of Russia: **Russia – Offices in Turkey.**

RL. PLATA F.: Cuba, Philippines.

RO on stamps of Turkey: **Eastern Rumelia.**

RODI: Italy – Aegean Islands – Rhodes.

ROMAGNE: Romagna.

ROMANA or **ROMINA: Romania.**

ROSS DEPENDENCY: New Zealand – Ross Dependency.

ROUMELIE ORIENTALE on stamps of Turkey: **Eastern Rumelia.**

ROYAUME DE L'ARABIE SAOUDITE: Saudi Arabia.

ROYAUME DE YEMEN: Yemen.

ROYAUME DU BURUNDI: Burundi.

ROYAUME DU CAMBODGE: Cambodia.

ROYAUME DU LAOS: Laos.

ROYAUME DU MAROC: Morocco.

RP (rappen): **Liechtenstein, Switzerland.**

R.P.E SHQIPERISE: Albania.

Rpf on stamps of Luxembourg: **Luxembourg – German occupation.**

R.P. ROMANIA: Romania.

R.R. with value in opposite corners: **Switzerland – Zurich.**

R.S.A.: South Africa.

R.S.M.: San Marino.

RUANDA on stamps inscribed "CONGO": **German East Africa – Belgian occupation.**

RUANDA-URUNDI on stamps of Congo Democratic Republic (ex-Belgian):
  Ruanda-Urundi.

73

RUMANIEN on stamps of Germany: **Romania – German occupation.**

RUSSISCH-POLEN on stamps of Germany: **Poland – German occupation.**

RUTHERFORDTON N.C.: United States – Rutherfordton, North Carolina.

RYUKYUS: Ryukyu Islands.

S

S on stamps of Straits Settlements: **Malay States – Selangor.**

S.A.: Saudi Arabia.

SAARE on stamps of Germany: **Saar.**

SAARGEBIET ("Saar Territory"): **Saar.**

SAARLAND, SAARPOST: Saar.

SABAH on stamps of North Borneo: **Sabah.**

SACHSEN: Saxony.

SAHARA ESPAÑOL or **SAHARA OCCIDENTAL: Spanish Sahara.**

ST. CHRISTOPHER-NEVIS-ANGUILLA: St. Kitts-Nevis.

SAINT LOUIS: United States – St. Louis, Missouri.

SAINT-PIERRE ET MIQUELON: St. Pierre and Miquelon.

S.A.K.: Saudi Arabia.

SALEM, N.C.: United States – Salem, North Carolina.

SALISBURY N.C.: United States – Salisbury, North Carolina.

SALONICCO on stamps of Italy: **Italy – Offices in Turkey – Salonica.**

SALONIQUE on stamps of Russia: **Russia – Offices in Turkey.**

SAMOA on stamps of Germany or New Zealand: **Samoa.**

SAN ANTONIO TEX.: United States – San Antonio, Texas.

SANDJAK D'ALEXANDRETTE on stamps of Syria: **Alexandretta.**

SANTANDER: Colombia – Saltander.

SAORSTAT ERIEANN ("Free State of Ireland") on stamps of Great Britain: **Ireland.**

SARKARI: India – Soruth.

SASENO on stamps of Italy: **Saseno.**

SAURASHTRA or **SOURRASHTRA: India – Soruth.**

SCARPANTO on stamps of Italy: **Italy – Aegean Islands – Scarpanto.**

SCHLESWIG: Schleswig-Holstein.

SCINDE DISTRIC DAWK: India – South District.

SCTARI DI ALBANIA on stamps of Italy: **Italy – Offices in Turkey – Scutari.**

SCUDO: Roman States.

SEGNA TASSA or **SEGNATASSE** with no country name: **Italy** – Postage due.

SEJM WILNIE: Central Lithuania.

SELANGOR: Malay States – Selangor.

SEN, SN.: Japan, Ryukyu Islands.

SENEGAL on stamps of French Colonies: **Senegal.**

SENEGAMBIE ET NIGER: Senegambia and Niger.

SERBIEN on stamps of Austria or Bosnia: **Serbia – Austrian occupation**; on stamps of Jugoslavia: **Serbia – German occupation.**

SERVICE: Official stamps of **India**, various Indian States, **Nepal, Pakistan.**

SERVICO POSTAL MEXICANA: Mexico.

SEVILLA-BARCELONA: Spain.

S.H.: Schleswig-Holstein.

SHANGHAI on stamps of United States: **United States – Offices in China.**

SHQIPENA, SHQIPENIAE, SHQIPENIE, SHQIPERIA, SHQIPERIE, SHQIPERIJA, SHQIPERISE, SHQIPTARE, SHQIPNI, SHQIPNIJA, SHQIPONIES, SHQYPNIS, SHQYPAARE: Albania.

S.H.S. (Abbreviation for "Serbs, Croats, Slovenes"): **Jugoslavia.**

SIEGE DE LA LIGUE ARABE: Morocco.

SIEGE OF MAFEKINF: Cape of Good Hope.

SIMI on stamps of Italy: **Italy – Aegean Islands – Simi.**

SINGAPORE MALAYA: Singapore.

SIRMOOR: India – Sirmoor.

SKILLING: Denmark, Norway.

SLD.: Austria – Offices in Turkey.

SLESVIG: Schleswig.

SLOVENSKA POSTA or **SLOVENSKO: Czechoslovakia – Slovakia.**

SLOVENSKY STAT, SLOVENSKENO on stamps of Czechoslovakia: **Czechoslovakia – Slovakia.**

S. MARINO: San Marino.

SMIRNE on stamps of Italy: **Italy – Offices in Turkey – Smyrna**; on stamps of Russia: **Russia – Offices in Turkey.**

S.O. 1920 on stamps of Czechoslovakia or Poland: **Eastern Silesia.**

SOBRETASA AREA: Colombia.

SOCIEDAD COLOMBIA-ALEMANA DE TRANSPORTES AEROEOS: Colombia.

SOCIEDADE DE GEOGRAPHIA DE LISBOA: Portugal.

SOCIETE DES NATIONS ("League of Nations"): **Switzerland – Official Stamps for the League of Nations.**

SOL: Peru.

SOLDI: Austria – Lombardy-Venetia.

SOLIDARITE FRANÇAISE: French Colonies.

SOMALIA on stamps of Italy: **Somalia.**

SOMALIA ITALIANA on stamps of Italy: **Somalia.**

SOMALI DEMOCRATIC REPUBLIC: Somalia.

SONORA: Mexico.

SOOMAALYA: Somalia

SORUTH: India – Soruth,

SOUDAN on stamps of Egypt: **Sudan**; on stamps of French Colonies: French Sudan.

SOUDAN FRANÇAIS: French Sudan.

SOURASHTRA: India – Soruth.

SOUTHERN RHODESIA on stamps of Great Britain: **Southern Rhodesia.**

SOUTH GEORGIA on stamps of Falkland Islands: **Falkland Islands Dependencies.**

SOUTH ORKNEYS on stamps of Falkland Islands: **Falkland Islands Dependencies.**

SOUTH SHETTLANDS on stamps of Falkland Islands: **Falkland Islands Dependencies.**

SOUTH WEST AFRICA on stamps of South Africa: **South-West Africa.**

SOWJETISCHE BESATZUGS ZONE on stamps of Germany: **Germany – Russian occupation.**

SPARTA GEO.: United States – Sparta, Georgia.

SPARTANBURO S.C.: United States – Spartanburg, South Carolina.

SPM on stamps of French Colonies: **St. Pierre and Miquelon.**

S.Q. TRSTA-UVJA: Trieste – Zone B.

SRODKOWA LITVA: Central Lithuania.

ST, STG ("satang"): Siam.

STAMPALIA on stamps of Italy: **Italy – Aegean Islands – Stampalia.**

STATE OF SINGAPORE: Singapore.

STATI PARM, or PARMEASI: Parma.

S. THOME E PRINCIPE: St. Thomas and Prince Islands.

STOCKHOLM: Sweden.

СТОТИНКИ: Bulgaria.

ST-PIERRE M-ON on stamps of French Colonies: **St. Pierre and Miquelon.**

STRAITS SETTLEMENTS on stamps of Labuan: **Straits Settlements.**

S.T. TRSTA-VUJA: Trieste – Zone B.

STT UVJA: Trieste – Zone B; on stamps of Jugoslavia: **Trieste – Zone B.**

S.U. on stamps of Straits Settlements: **Malay States – Sungei Ujong.**

SUIDAFRIKA: South Africa.

SUIDWES AFRIKA: South-West Africa.

S. UJONG: Malay States – Sungei Ujong.

SUL BOLLETTINO or **SULLA RICEVUTA: Italy**, unless additionally
overprinted for the various Italian Colonies; on
stamps with star and crescent emblem: **Somalia.**

SULTANT D'ANJOUAN: Anjouan.

SULTANATE OF OMAN on stamps of Muscat and Oman: **Oman.**

SUNGEI UJONG: Malay States – Sungei Ujong.

SUOMI: Finland.

SURINAME: Surinam.

SVERIGE: Sweden.

S.W.A. South-West Africa.

SWAZIELAND Swaziland.

SWAZILAND on stamps of South Africa: **Swaziland.**

SYRIAN ARAB REPUBLIC: Syria.

SYRIE, SYRIENNE: Syria.

T

T: Belgium; in four courners of stamp, with numeral in center:
Dominican Republic; inclosed in a circle: **Peru –
Huacho.**

TAHITI on stamps of French Colonies: **Tahiti.**

TAKCA: Bulgaria.

TAKSE: Albania.

TALBOTTON GA.: United States – Talbotton, Georgia.

TANGANYIKA, KENYA, UGANDA: Kenya, Uganda and Tanzania.

TANGANYIKA ZANZIBAR: Tanzania.

TANGER with "Correo Espanol": **Spanish Morocco – Tangier**; on
stamps of France: **French Morocco**;
on stamps of Great Britain:
Great Britain – Offices in Morocco.

TANZANIA, KENYA, UGANDA: Kenya, Uganda and Tanzania.

TASSE GAZZETTE: Modena.

TAXA DE GUERRA ("War tax") with value in AVOS: **Macao**; with
value in OS: **Portuguese Africa**; with values in RP:
Portuguese India; with values in REIS: **Portuguese
Guinea.**

TAXE: Albania.

TC on stamps of India or Cochin: **India – Travancore – Chochin.**

T.C.E.K.: Turkey.

TCHAD: Chad.

TCHONGKING on stamps of Indo-China: **France – Offices in China -
Tchong King.**

T.C. POSTALARI: Turkey.

TE BETALEN: Dutch Indies, Netherlands, Netherlands Antilles, Suriname; preceded by "A PAYER": **Belgium.**

TE BETALEN PORT on red or carmine stamps: **Dutch Indies**; on vermilion stamps: **Dutch New Guinea**; on blue stamps: **Netherlands**; on green stamps: **Netherlands Antilles**; on lilac or purple stamps: **Surinam.**

TELLICO PLAINS TENN.: United States – Tellico Plains, Tennessee.

T.E.O. ("Occupied Territories of the Enemy") with denominations in MILLEMES on stamps of France: **Syria**; on stamps of France – Offices in Turkey: **Cilicia,**

TERRES AUSTRALES ET ANTARCTIQUES FRANÇISES: French Southern and Antartic Territories.

TERRITOIRE DE IFNI on stamps of Spain: **Ifni.**

TERRITOIRE DE'ININI: Inini.

TERRITOIRE DU FEZZAN: Libya – Fezzan – French occupation.

TERRITOIRE DU NIGER: Niger.

TERRITOIRE FRANÇAIS DES AFARS ET ISSAS: Affars and Issas.

TERRITORIO DE IFNI (ESPAÑA): Ifni.

TERRITORIOS DEL AFRICA OCCIDENTAL ESPAÑOLA: Spanish West Africa.

TERRITORIOS or **TERRS. ESPAÑOLES DEL GOLFO DE GUINEA: Spanish Guinea.**

TETUAN: Spanish Morocco – Tetuan.

THAILAND or **THAI: Siam.**

THAILAND with values in cents: **Malaya – Siamese occupation.**

THOMASVILLE GA.: United States – Thomasville, Georgia.

THRACE INTERALLIEE or **THRACE OCCIDENTAL** on stamps of Bulgaria: **Thrace.**

TIENTSIN on stamps of Italy: **Italy – Offices in China – Tien Tsin.**

TIMBE IMPERIAL JOURNAUX: France.

TIMBER POSTE on stamps of France: **French Morocco.**

TIMBRE TAXE with numeral and no country name: **French Colonies.**

TIMOR on stamps of Macao or Mozambique: **Timor.**

TJENESTEFIRMERKE: Norway.

TJENEST-FRIMARKE: Denmark.

TOGA: Tonga.

TOGO on stamps of Dahomey, Germany or Gold Coast: **Togo.**

TOLIMA: Colombia – Tolima.

TO PAY: Great Britain – Postage due.

TOSCONO: Tuscany.

TOU.: Persia.

TOUVA: Tannu Tuva.

TRAITE DE VERSAILLES: Allenstein.

TRANS-JORDAN: Jordan.

TRANSPORTO PACCHI IN CONCESSIONE: Italy –Authorized delivery stamps.

TRAVANCORE: India – Travancore.

TRAVANCORE-COCHIN: India – Travancore-Cochin.

TREBIZONDE on stamps of Russia: **Russia – Offices in Turkey.**

TRENGGANU: Malay States – Tregganu.

TRIPOLI: Tripolitania; preceded by "FIERA CAMPIONARIA": **Libya.**

TRIPOLI DI BARBERIA on stamps of Italy: **Italy – Offices in Africa – Tripoli.**

TRIPOLITANIA on stamps of Italy: **Tripolitania.**

TRISTAN DA CUNHA on stamps of St. Helena: **Tristan da Cunha.**

T. Ta. C.: Turkey.

TULLAHOMA TEN.: United States – Tullahoma, Tennessee.

TUNIS, TUNISIE: Tunisia.

TURKIYE CUMHURIYETI: Turkey.

TURKIYE, TURK POSTALARI: Turkey.

TUSCUMBIA: United States – Tuscumbia, Alabama.

TUSCUMBIA ALA: United States – Tuscumbia, Alabama.

T. WELSH: United States – Montgomery, Alabama.

TWO PENCE under an enthroned queen: **Victoria.**

U

ЦАРСТВО: Bulgaria.

ЦАРСТВО БЪЛГАРИЯ: Bulgaria.

U.A.R. (United Arab Republic) with values in "M" or " £ ": **Egypt;** with values in "P": **Syria – United Arab Republic.**

U.G.: Uganda.

UGANDA on stamps of British East Africa: **Uganda.**

UGANDA, KENYA, TANGANYIKA: Kenya, Uganda and Tanzania.

UGANDA, KENYA, TANZANIA: Kenya, Uganda and Tanzania.

UKRAINE on stamps of Germany: **Russia – German occupation.**

ULTRAMAR ("Beyond the Sea") with a year date: **Cuba, Puerto Rico**; with denominations in "AVOS" or "REIS": **Guniea, Macao.**

UNEF on stamps of India: **India – Military stamps – Gaza.**

U.N. FORCE (INDIA) CONGO on stamps of India: **India – Military stamps – Congo.**

UNION CITY, TENNESSEE: United States – Union City, Tennessee.

UNITED ARAB EMIRATES on stamps of Abu Dhabi: **United Arab Emirates.**

UNTEA on stamps of Dutch New Guinea: West New Guinea.

UOPTO ОКРИСОРИ: Romania – Moldavia.

ЦРНА ГОРА: Montenegro – Italian occupation.

URUNDI on stamps of Congo Democratic Republic (ex-Belgian):
German East Africa – Belgian occupation.

US or U.S.A.: United States.

U.S. PENNY POST: United States – St. Louis, Missouri.

U.S.P.O.: United States.

V

VALDOSTA GA.: United States – Valdosta, Georgia.

VALLEES D'ANDORRE: Andorra.

VALONA on stamps of Italy: Italy – Officies in Turkey.

VALPARAISO MULTADO: Chile.

VANCOUVER ISLAND: British Colombia and Vancouver Island.

VAN DIEMEN'S LAND: Tasmania.

VATHY: France – Officies in Turkey.

VATICANE or VATICANA: Vatican City.

VENEZIA GIULIA, VENEZIA TRIDENTINA on stamps of Austria or
Italy: Austria – Italian occupation.

VENZ, VENSOLANO: Venezuela.

VICTORIA: United States – Victoria, Texas.

VIET-NAM CONG-HOA: Viet Nam.

VIVA ESPAÑA CORRES AERO on stamps of Spain: Spain – various
states.

VOJNA UPRAVA JUGOSLAVENSKE ARMIJE on stamps of Jugoslavia:
Jugoslavia – Issues for Istria and the Slovene Coast.

VOM EMPFANGER EINŻUZIEMEN: Danzig.

V.R. SPECIAL POST on stamps of Transvaal: Cape of Good Hope.

VUJA STT or VUJNA STT on stamps of Jugoslavia: Trieste – Zone B.

W

WADHWAN: India – Wadhwan.

WARRENTON GA.: United States – Warrenton, Georgia.

W. AUSTRALIA: Western Australia.

W.D. COLEMAN: United States – Danville, Virginia.

WENDENSCHNE: Russia – Wenden.

WEST AUSTRALIA: Western Australia.

WESTERN SAMOA: Samoa.

WHARTON'S: United States – Louisville, Kentucky.

WILLIAMS: United States – Cincinnati, Ohio.

WINNSBOROUGH S.C.: United States – Winnsbourgh, South Carolina.

WN ("weun"): **Korea.**
WURTTEMBERG: Germany – Wurttemberg – French occupation, Wurttemberg.
WYTHEVILLE VA: United States – Wytheville, Virginia.

X

ΧΑΡΤΟΣΗΜΟΝ: **Greece.**
XEJEPA: **Montenegro.**
ΧΕΛΕΡΑ: **Montenegro.**
XII CAMPIONARIA TRIPOLI ("12th Tripolitan Fair"): **Libya.**

Y

YCA on stamps of Peru: **Peru – Yca.**
У.С.С.Р.: **Ukraine**; on stamps of Russia: **Ukraine.**
YCTAB: **Montenegro.**
YEN, YN.: **Japan, Manchuko, Ryukyu Islands.**
YKP on stamps of Austria: **Western Ukraine.**
УКРАІНСЬКА: **Ukraine.**
YUNNAN FOU on stamps of Indo-China: **France – Officies in China –
        Yunnan Fou.**
YUNNANSEN on stamps of Indo-China: **France – Officies in China –
        Yunnan Fou.**

Z

Z. AFR. REPUBLIEK, ZUID AFRIKAANSCHE REPUBLIEK ("South African
        Republic"): **Transvaal.**
ZANZIBAR on stamps of France: **France – Officies in Zanzibar**;
        on stamps of British East Africa or India: **Zanzibar.**
ZANZIBAR TANZANIA: **Zanzibar.**
ZEGELREGT: **Transvaal.**
ZELAYA: **Nicaragua – Zelaya.**
ZENTRALER KURIERDIENST: **Germany – German Democratic Republic.**
ZONA DE OCUPATIE ROMANIA on stamps of Hungary: **Hungary – Roumanian
        occupation.**
ZONA PROTECTORADO ESPAÑOL on stamps of Spain: **Spanish Morocco.**
ZONE FRANÇAISE: **Germany – French occupation.**
ZRACNA POSTA: **Trieste – Zone B.**
ZUIDWEST AFRIKA: **South West Africa.**
ZULULAND on stamps of Great Britain or Natal: **Zululand.**
ZURICH: **Switzerland.**

HOW TO COLLECT STAMPS

3.y.H.B. on stamps of Austria: **Western Ukraine.**

ПАРА, ПАРЕ: Montenegro, Serbia.

ПОРТО МАРКА: Serbia.

ПОУТА: Russia.

গ ণ প্ৰ জা ত ন্ত্ৰী : **Bangladesh.**

OTHER HARD-TO-IDENTIFY STAMPS

A class of stamps very difficult to identify are those which are not inscribed with any recognizable words and therefore cannot be indexed in the preceding word-list. Such stamps should be checked in this section of STAMP IDENTIFIER.

It is impossible, because of limited space to illustrate all stamps of this kind. We have tried to show a sufficient number so that you can identify virtually all of the others.

AFGHANISTAN

Tiger's head and crudely drawn mosque encircled in wreath or ornament identify many of the early issues.

ARMENIA

ARMENIA

Inscription resembling "ZULZ" and "N.F.L." and national emblem – a star, sometimes enclosing a hammer and sickle – identify many stamps of Armenia.

AUSTRIA

84

AZERBAIJAN

BANGLADESH

BATUM

BOSNIA & HERZEGOVINA

These stamps, if imperforate, belong under Bosnia & Herzegovina; if perforate, under Jugoslavia.

ДРЖАВА С. Х. С.
Босна и Херцеговина === JUGOSLAVIA

BRAZIL

BULGARIA

БЪЛГАРИЯ   БЪЛГАРСКА

overprinted: **ROMANIA** — Bulgarian Occupation

Поща въ Ромъния 1916—1917

BURMA
under Japanese Occupation

overprinted:
under
Japanese Occupation

HOW TO COLLECT STAMPS

CHINA

The typical Chinese characters, and the sun emblem in a circle, identify many stamps of China.

87

CRETE

ΛΕΠΤΑ. ΛΕΠΤΟΝ   ΠΡΟΣΩΡΙΝΟΝ

Δ Ρ.. ΔΡΑΧΜΗ   ΜΕΤΑΛΛΙΚ

ΕΛΛΑΣ

CUBA
under Spanish Dominion

overprinted: PUERTO RICO

NETHERLANDS INDIES

Under Japanese Occupation

88

EGYPT

EPIRUS ·

ΛΕΠΤΑ..ΛΕΠΤΟΝ

ΗΠΕΙΡΟΣ

ΔΡ.. ΔΡΑΧΜΗ

ETHIOPIA

FAR EASTERN REPUBLIC
ПОЧТОВАЯ МАРКА

HOW TO COLLECT STAMPS

FAR EASTERN REPUBLIC

overprinted:

SIBERIA

FINLAND

ПОЧТОВАЯ МАРКА

FRENCH   COLONIES

2 CENTS

— Offices in China

5

— French Morocco

FRANCE

The stamps shown, if perforated, are France, if imperforate, French Colonies. The stamp shown is French Colonies.

FRENCH COLONIES

Stamps of the type shown were issued for general use in all the French Colonies. To suit local postal needs, various colonies surcharged these stamps with new denominations. The surcharged issues were thereafter classified under the heading of the colony which surcharged and used them. Each colony's surcharges were printed in a characteristic style of type as shown. In some cases denominations additional to those pictured here were used but the style of type remains constant and makes identification possible.

overprinted:

REUNION   Annam and Tonkin

GERMANY

overprinted: FRANCE under German Occupation

AUSTRIA   Lothringen   Elſaß

overprinted: POLAND under German Occupation

Ruſſiſch-
Polen   Gen.-Gonv
Warſchau

GERMANY

overprinted: ROMANIA under German Occupation

N.V.i.R
25 Bani

Rumänien
25 Bani

GEORGIA

GREAT BRITAIN

overprinted:
IRELAND

Rialtar
Sealadac
na
hÉireann
1922

Saorstat
Éireann
1922

overprinted: OMAN

2½ ANNAS | 2 RUPEES | 1 ANNA

GREECE

ΕΛΛΑΣ   ΔΡ.. ΔΡΑΧΜΗ

ΛΕΠΤΑ. ΛΕΠΤΟΝ

HOW TO COLLECT STAMPS

GREECE

overprinted: THRACE

Διοίκησις
Δυτικῆς
Θράκης

HUNGARY

INDIA — Gwalior   **INDIA**   MUSCAT

INDIA NATIVE STATES

ALWAR   BHOPAL   BUNDI   overprinted:
Rajasthan

DHAR   FARIDKOT   JAMMU & KASHMIR

HOW TO COLLECT STAMPS

INDIAN NATIVE STATES

JASDAN JHALAWAR KISHANGARH RAJPEEPLA

JHIND

NANDGAON POONCH NOWANUGGUR

IRELAND

ISRAEL

JAPAN

A stylized chrysanthemum, the national emblem of Imperial Japan was included in virtually all stamp designs produced by this country through 1947. Nearly all subsequent issues bear the name of Japan in four Japanese characters, arranged either vertically or horizontally.

94

HOW TO COLLECT STAMPS

JAPAN

HONG KONG	NORTH BORNEO	KOREA under
under Japanese Occupation	under	U S MILITARY
	Japanese/Occupation	Rule

 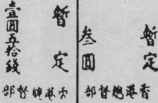

JORDAN

KOREA

 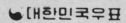 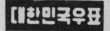

The national emblem of Korea and the characteristic letters after the initials "CH" will enable you to identify most issues.

LEBANON

LIBYA

LOURENCO MARQUES

overprinted:

10 c.

MOZAMBIQUE

MALAYA

under Japanese Occupation

MALAY STATES

Kelantan Pahang Perak

Negri Sembilan Selangor Trengganu

MANCHUKUO

MAURITANIA

5 fr. ═

overprinted:

FRENCH WEST AFRICA

97

MONGOLIA

MONTENEGRO

ПОШТЕ П РНЕГОРЕ   ПАРА , ПАРЕ
ХЕЛЕР

NEPAL

98

PAKISTAN

PAKISTAN
Bahawalpur

PALESTINE

overprinted:

TRANS-JORDAN

PANAMA

PERSIA (IRAN)

The heraldic lion brandishing a sword before the rising sun in the national emblem of Persia and identifies many early issues. Many later issues of Persia may be identified by the Arabic lettering shown in the lower central portion of the last stamp pictured.

PHILIPPINES
under Japanese Occupation

RUSSIA

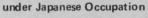

ПОЧТОВАЯ МАРКА Р.С.Ф.С.Р.

All Russian stamps issued since 1922 bear the initials
"C C C P", the Russian abbreviation for "Union of Soviet Socialist Republics".

RUSSIA
overprinted:
ARMENIA

к 60 к

10 г   5 г

г.5000 г.

FAR EASTERN REPUBLIC

Д.   В.
коп. 1 коп.
ЗОЛОТОМ

SIBERIA

Прид.
Земскій
Край

GEORGIA

15.000 эзб

200 000
эзб.

SOUTH RUSSIA

25	1 р.	70 коп.	10 рублей
—25	—1 р.		—70 к.

5

пять

рублей.

35 коп.

— 3 —

рубля

TRANSCAUCASIAN FEDERATED REPUBLICS

700 000 руб.

RUSSIA
overprinted:

Р.О.П.иТ.

UKRAINE

35 к.

How to Indentify Early
Issues of Russia and Finland

Stamps of Finland are identical to stamps of Russia except for the dots in circles worked into background.

Stamps of Finland are lettered for Finnish currency, penna and markaa. Closely similar Russian stamps are lettered for Kopecks and rubles.

RYUKYU ISLANDS

The country named in its own language, arranged horizontally or vertically as shown, and denominations in $ and ¢, will identify most of the issues.

SAUDI ARABIA

SAUDI ARABIA   HEJAZ

SAUDI ARABIA
overprinted:
NEJD

SAUDI ARABIA   overprinted: TRANS-JORDAN

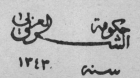

SAUDI ARABIA—Nejd

overprinted:

TRANS-JORDAN

كومة	فنفج	حكومة
النرق العربية	مالك العرب	حكومة النرق العربية
مستقيق	اج ب ٢٢ جالغنة	٥ تبار ١٠٠
٩ نيسان ١٣٤١م	١ اج ب ٢٢ جالغنة	

حكومة النرق
العربي
١٣٤٢

SENEGAL   overprinted: FRENCH WEST AFRICA

50 fr.

=

SERBIA

ПАРА, ПАРЕ   СРПСКА   СРВИЈА

overprinted: JUGOSLAVIA

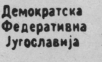

+ 3   =

HOW TO COLLECT STAMPS

SIAM (Thailand)

SIBERIA

overprinted:

FAR EASTERN REPUBLIC

SOUTH RUSSIA

SWITZERLAND

SYRIA

SYRIA

overprinted
UNITED ARAB REPUBLIC

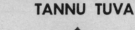

TANNU TUVA

THRACE ΘΡΑΚΗΣ. Θραχης

TRANSCAUCASIAN FEDERATED REPUBLICS
З.С.Ф.С.Р.

TURKEY

Many early issues of Turkey are identified by the "tughra" or sultan's monogram or by the star and crescent, Turkish national emblem. But – caution! – the star and crescent is also the national emblem of Tunisia and of Pakistan; and the tughra appears on some of the early issues of Saudi Arabia.

TURKEY

GREECE   overprinted: — Mytilene

Ἑλληνικὴ
Κατοχή
Μυτιλήνης

overprinted: THRACE

Υπάτη Αρμοστεία
Θραχης
5 Λεπτὰ 5

overprinted: SYRIA

SAUDI ARABIA
overprinted:

— Nejd

UKRAINE

НАРОДНЯ-РЕСПУЂЛІКА

The UNITED STATES
Stamp Identifier

SHOWS YOU HOW TO DISTINGUISH BETWEEN THE

RARE AND COMMON UNITED STATES STAMPS THAT LOOK ALIKE

What does "Grill with points up" mean? "Single line water-mark"? How can I tell whether my 15¢ "Landing of Columbus" stamp of 1869 is worth $1175.00 (Type 1) or only $600.00 (Type II)?

At one time or another, every collector of United States stamps asks questions like these. For very often it is a minute difference in design that determines not only whether a stamp is Type I, II or III, but whether it is a great rarity or just another common variety. The different varieties of the 1¢ Franklin design of 1851-57, for example, range in price from $22.50 to $75,000! So it pays to know how to tell the correct types of your stamps! To enable you to do so easily and quickly is the purpose of this U.S. STAMP IDENTIFIER.

Other seemingly identical, but actually different United States stamps may be told apart by differences in perforations, water-marks, grills or methods of printing. These terms are fully explained in the glossary at the back of this IDENTIFIER. And charts are included which make it easy for you to quickly identify the most troublesome of all U.S. stamps – the hard-to-classify regular issues of 1908 to 1932.

FIRST UNITED STATES POSTAGE ISSUE OF 1847

The first stamps of the United States Government – the 5¢ and 10¢ designs shown to the left above – were placed in use in July 1847, superseding the Postmasters' Provisionals then being used in several cities. In 1875, official reproductions (next page) were made from newly engraved printing plates.

NOTE: The illustrations and catalog numbers used herein are from the Standard Postage Stamp Catalogue, by special permission of the publishers, Scott Publications, Inc.

In the original 5¢ design, the top edge of Franklin's shirt touches the circular frame about at a level with the top of the "F" of "FIVE", while in the 1875 reproduction it is on a level with the top of the figure "5".

In the original 10¢ design, the left edge of Washington's coat points to the "T" of "TEN", and the right edge points between the "T" and "S" of "CENTS". In the reproductions, the left and right outlines of the coat point to the right edge of "X" and to the center of the "S" of "CENTS" respectively. Also, on the 1875 reprints, the eyes have a sleepy look and the line of the mouth is straighter.

The 1947 "Cipex" Souvenir Sheet, issued on the hundredth anniversary of United States stamps, features reproductions of the two original designs. Stamps cut out of the souvenir sheet are, of course, valid for postage. However, no difficulty in identification should be encountered since the 1947 reproductions are light blue (5¢) instead of the original red brown, and brownish orange (10¢) instead of the original black.

TYPES OF THE 1c FRANKLIN DESIGN OF 1851-61

TYPE I has the most complete design of the various types of this stamp. At top and bottom there is an unbroken curved line running outside the bands reading "U.S. POSTAGE" and "ONE CENT". The scrolls at bottom are turned under, forming curls. The scrolls and outer line at top are complete.

TYPE Ia is like Type I at bottom but ornaments and curved line at top are partly cut away.

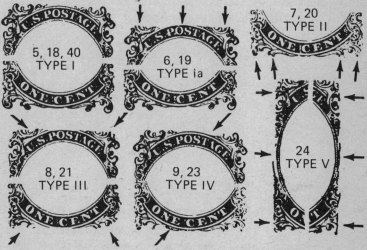

TYPE Ib (not illustrated) is like Type I at top but little curls at bottom are not quite so complete nor clear and scroll work is partly cut away.

TYPE II has the outside bottom line complete, but the little curls of the bottom scrolls and the lower part of the plume ornaments are missing. Side ornaments are complete.

TYPE III has the outside lines at both top and bottom partly cut away in the middle. The side ornaments are complete.

TYPE IIIa (not illustrated) is similar to Type III with the outer line cut away at top or bottom, but not both. 8A, 22.

TYPE IV is similar to Type II but the curved lines at top or bottom (or both) have been recut in several different ways, and usually appear thicker than Type IIs.

TYPE V is similar to Type III but has the side ornaments partly cut away. Type V occurs only on perforated stamps.

TYPES OF THE 3¢ WASHINGTON DESIGN OF 1851-61

26
Type II

26a
Type IIa

TYPE I has a frame line around the top, bottom and sides.
TYPE II has the frame line removed at top and bottom, while the side frame lines are continuous from top to bottom of the plate.

TYPE IIa is similar to Type II, but the side frame lines were recut individually, hence are broken between stamps.

TYPES OF THE 5¢ JEFFERSON DESIGN OF 1851-61

12, 27–29
Type I

30, 30A, 42
Type II

TYPE I is a complete design with projections (arrow) at the top and bottom as well as at the sides.
TYPE II has the projections at the top and bottom partly or completely cut away.

TYPES OF THE 10¢ WASHINGTON DESIGN OF 1851-61

TYPE I has the "shells" at the lower corners practically complete, while the outer line below "TEN CENTS" is very nearly complete. At the top, the outer lines are broken above "U.S. POSTAGE" and above the "X" in each corner.

TYPE II has the design complete at the top, but the outer line at the bottom is broken in the middle and the "shells" are partially cut away.

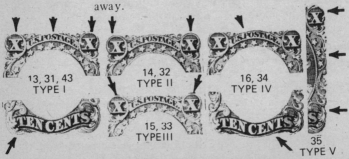

13, 31, 43
TYPE I

14, 32
TYPE II

15, 33
TYPE III

16, 34
TYPE IV

35
TYPE V

112

TYPE III has both top and bottom outer lines partly cut away; that is, similar to Type I at the top and Type II at the bottom.

TYPE IV has the outer lines at the top or bottom of the stamp, or at both places, recut to show more strongly and heavily.
Types I, II, III and IV have complete ornaments at the sides and three small circles or pearls at the outer edges of the bottom panel.

TYPE V has the side ornaments, including one or two of the small "pearls" partly cut away. The outside line over the "X" at the right top has also been partly cut away.

TYPES OF THE ISSUE OF 1861

Shortly after the outbreak of the Civil War in 1861, the Post Office demonetized all stamps issued up to that time in order to prevent their use by the Confederacy. Two new sets of designs, consisting of the six stamps shown above plus 24¢ and 30¢ denominations, were prepared by the American Bank Note Company. The first designs, except for the 10¢ and 24¢ values, were not regularly issued and are extremely rare and valuable. The second designs became the regular issue of 1861. The illustrations at the left below show the first (or un-issued) designs, which were all printed on thin, semi-transparent paper. The second (or regular) designs are shown at the right.

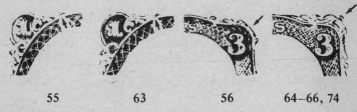

55   63   56   64–66, 74

63 shows a small dash (arrow) under the tip of the ornaments at the right of the figure "1" in the upper left hand corner of the stamp.

64, 66 and **74** show a small ball (arrow) at each corner of the design. Also, the ornaments at the corners are larger than on 56.

3¢ 1861 PINK (Scott's #64) — It is impossible to describe a "pink" in words, but it might be helpful to remember that this stamp is usually rather heavily inked, and has a tinge of blue or purple which makes it stand out from the various shades of rose to red brown sometimes mistaken for it.

57   67, 75, 76

59   69

67, 75 and 76 have a leaflet (arrow) projecting from the scrolled ornaments at each corner of the stamp.

69 has an oval and scroll (arrow) in each corner of the design. 59 has no such design and the corners are rounded.

58, 62B   68

62   72

58, 62B has no curved line below the row of stars and there is only one outer line of the ornaments above them.

68 has a heavy curved line below the row of stars (arrow), and the ornaments above the stars have a double outer line.

62 does not have the row of dashes or spot of color present in 72.

72 has a row of small dashes between the parallel lines of the angle at the top center of the stamp. There is also a spot of color (arrow) in the apex of the lower line of the angle.

TYPES OF THE 15¢ "LANDING OF COLUMBUS" DESIGN OF 1869

118: Type I

119: Type II

118, TYPE I ,has the central picture without the frame line shown in Type II.

119, TYPE II, has a frame line around   central picture; also a diamond shaped ornament appears below the "T" of "POST-AGE".

129, TYPE III (not illustrated) is like Type I except that the fringe of brown shading lines which appears around the sides and bottom of the picture on Types I and II has been removed.

TYPES OF THE 1870-71 AND 1873 ISSUES

The stamps of the 1870-71 issue were printed by the National Bank Note Company. The similar issue of 1873 was printed by the Continental Bank Note Company. When Continental took over the plates previously used by National, they applied the so-called "secret marks" to the designs of the 1¢ through 15¢ denominations, by which the two issues can be distinguished as shown below. The illustrations show the original designs of 1870-71, and the secret marks applied to the issue of 1873.

134, 135   156

156 has a small curved mark in the pearl at the left of the figure "1".

137, 148   159

159 has the first four vertical lines of shading in the lower part of the left ribbon greatly strengthened.

135, 146   157

135 and 146 are red brown. Type 157 is brown and in some copies has a small diagonal line under the scroll at the left of the "U.S." (arrow).

138, 149   160

160 has two tiny semicircles drawn around the end of the lines which outline the ball in the ball in the lower right hand corner.

136, 147   158

158 has the ribbon under the letters "RE" heavily shaded.

139, 150   161

161 has a small semicircle in the scroll at the righthand side of the central design.

140, 151

162 has the "balls" at the top and bottom of the figure "2". crescent-shaped instead of nearly round as in 140 and 151.

141, 152

163 has strengthened lines (arrow) in the triangle in the upper left-hand corner, forming a "V".

RE-ENGRAVED DESIGNS OF 1881-82

The 1c, 3c, 6c, and 10c denominations of the 1873 & 1879 issues, shown above, were re-engraved in 1881-82. The new plates resulted in the four variations described below. The background shading lines in all four of these stamps appear stronger and more heavily inked than the earlier designs.

206 has strengthened vertical shading lines in the upper part of the stamp, making the background appear almost solid. Lines of shading have also been added to the curving ornaments in the upper corners.

207 has a solid shading line at the sides of the central oval (arrow) that is only about half the previous width. Also a short horizontal line has been cut below the "TS" of "CENTS".

209 has only four vertical lines between the left side of the oval and the edge of the shield. (In the preceding issues there were five such lines.) Also, the lines in the background have been made much heavier so that these stamps appear more heavily inked than previous issues.

208 has only three vertical lines between the edge of the panel and the outside left margin of the stamp; (In the preceding issues there were four such lines.)

TYPES OF THE REGULAR ISSUES OF 1890-98

1890-93. This issue, printed by the American Bank Note Company, consists of a 1¢, 2¢, 3¢, 4¢, 5¢, 6¢, 8¢, 10¢, 15¢, 30¢, and 90¢, denomination.

1894-98. This issue – and all subsequent regular United States issues – were printed by the Bureau of Engraving and Printing, Washington, D.C. In more recent years, starting in 1943, some commemorative issues were printed by private firms. The 1894-98 "Bureau" issue is similar in design to the issue of 1890 but triangles (arrows) were added to the upper corners of the stamps and there are some differences in denominations.

2¢ "CAP ON 2" VARIETY OF 1890

Plate defects in the printing of the 2c "Washington" stamp of 1890 account for the "Cap on left 2" and "Cap on both 2s" varieties illustrated above.

TYPES OF THE 2¢ WASHINGTON DESIGN OF 1894-98

265
248–250,
Type I

251, 266
Type II

279B
252, 267,
Type III

The triangles in the upper right and left hand corners of the stamp determine the type.

TYPE I has horizontal lines of the same thickness within and without the triangle.

TYPE II has horizontal lines which cross the triangle but are thinner within it than without.

TYPE III has thin lines inside the triangle and these do not cross the double frame line of the triangle.

10¢ WEBSTER DESIGN OF 1898

TYPE I has an unbroken white curved line below the words "TEN CENTS".

In **TYPE II** the white line is broken by the ornaments at a point just below the "E" in "TEN" and the "F" in "CENTS" (arrows).

Type I   Type II

$1 PERRY DESIGN OF 1894-95

Type I   Type II

In **TYPE I** the circles around the "$1" are broken at the point where they meet the curved line below "ONE DOLLAR" (arrows). **TYPE II** shows these circles complete.

2¢ COLUMBIAN "BROKEN HAT" VARIETY OF 1893

As a result of a plate defect, some stamps of the 2c Columbian design show a noticeable white notch or gash in the hat worn by the third figure to the left of Columbus. This "broken hat" variety is somewhat less common than the regular 2c design.

4¢ COLUMBIAN BLUE ERROR — Collectors often mistake the many shades of the normal 4¢ ultramarine for the rare and valuable blue error. Actually, the "error" is not ultramarine at all, but a deep blue, similar to the deeper blue shades of the 1¢ Columbian.

HOW TO USE THE FOLLOWING IDENTIFICATION CHARTS

22mm Size of Flat Plate Design

18½-19mm

Stamps printed by rotary press are always slightly wider or taller on issues prior to 1954. Measurements do not apply to booklet singles.

Numbers referred to herein are from Scott's Standard Postage Stamp Catalog. To identify any stamp in this series, first check the type by comparing it with the illustrations at the top of the chart. Then check the perforations, and whether the stamp is single or double line watermarked or unwatermarked. With this information you can quickly find out the Standard Catalog number by checking down and across the chart. For example, a 1¢ Franklin, perf. 12, single line watermark, must be Scott's #374.

FRANKLIN AND WASHINGTON ISSUES OF 1908-22

Perforation	Watermark	Other Identifying Features	One Cent	Two Cents
PERF. 12	USPS	White paper	331	332
		Bluish grey paper	357	358
	USPS	White paper	374	375
COIL 12	USPS	Perf. Horizontal	348	349
		Perf. Vertical	352	353
	USPS	Perf. Horizontal	385	386
		Perf. Vertical	387	388
IMPERF.	USPS		343	344
	USPS	Flat Plate	383	384
		Rotary Press		
	Unwmkd	Flat Plate		
		Offset		
COIL 8½	USPS	Perf. Horizontal	390	391
		Perf. Vertical	392	393
PERF. 10	USPS			
	USPS			
	Unwmkd	Flat Plate		
		Rotary Press		
COIL 10	USPS	Perf. Horiz. Flat		
		Perf. Horiz. Rotary		
		Perf. Vert. Flat		
		Perf. Vert. Rotary		
	Unwmkd	Perf. Horizontal		
		Perf. Vertical		
PERF. 11	USPS			519
	USPS			
	Unwmkd	Flat Plate		
		Rotary Press		
		Offset		
12½	Unwmkd	Offset		
11x10	Unwmkd	Rotary		
10x11	Unwmkd	Rotary		

FRANKLIN AND WASHINGTON ISSUES OF 1908-22

Perforation	Watermark	Other Identifying Features	1¢	2¢
PERF. 12	USPS	White paper		
		Bluish grey paper		
	USPS	White paper	405	406
COIL 12	USPS	Perf. Horizontal		
		Perf. Vertical		
	USPS	Perf. Horizontal		
		Perf. Vertical		
IMPERF.	USPS			
	USPS	Flat Plate	408	409
		Rotary Press		459
	Unwmkd	Flat Plate	481	482-82 A
		Offset	531	532-34B
COIL 8½	USPS	Perf. Horizontal	410	411
		Perf. Vertical	412	413
PERF. 10	USPS			
	USPS		424	425
	Unwmkd	Flat Plate	462	463
		Rotary Press	543	
COIL 10	USPS	Perf. Horiz. Flat	441	442
		Perf. Horiz. Rotary	448	449-50
		Perf. Vert. Flat	443	444
		Perf. Vert. Rotary	452	453-55
	Unwmkd	Perf. Horizontal	486	487-88
		Perf. Vertical	490	491-92
PERF. 11	USPS			
	USPS			461
	Unwmkd	Flat Plate	498	499-500
		Rotary Press	*544-45	546
		Offset	525	526-28B
12½	Unwmkd	Offset	536	
11x10	Unwmkd	Rotary	538	539-40
10x11	Unwmkd	Rotary	542	

*Design of #544 is 19 mm. wide x 22½ mm. high. #545 is 19½ to 20 mm. wide x 22 mm. high.

FRANKLIN AND WASHINGTON ISSUES OF 1908-22

Perforation	Watermark	Other Identifying Features	3c thru $1 Denominations	8c thru $1 Denominations
PERF. 12	USPS	White paper	333-42	422-23
	USPS	Bluish grey paper	359-66	
	USPS	White paper	376-82,407	414-21
COIL 12	USPS	Perf. Horizontal	350-51	
	USPS	Perf. Vertical	354-56	
	USPS	Perf. Horizontal		
	USPS	Perf. Vertical	389	
IMPERF.	USPS		345-47	
	USPS	Flat Plate		
	USPS	Rotary Press		
	Unwmkd	Flat Plate	483-84	
	Unwmkd	Offset	535	
COIL 8½	USPS	Perf. Horizontal		
	USPS	Perf. Vertical	394-96	
PERF. 10	USPS			460
	USPS		426-30	431-40
	Unwmkd	Flat Plate	464-69	470-78
	Unwmkd	Rotary Press		
COIL 10	USPS	Perf. Horiz. — Flat		
	USPS	Perf. Horiz. — Rotary		
	USPS	Perf. Vert. — Flat	445-47	
	USPS	Perf. Vert. — Rotary	456-58	
	Unwmkd	Perf. Horizontal	489	
	Unwmkd	Perf. Vertical	493-96	497
PERF. 11	USPS			
	USPS			
	Unwmkd	Flat Plate	501-07	508-18
	Unwmkd	Rotary Press		
	Unwmkd	Offset	529-30	
12½	Unwmkd	Offset		
11x10	Unwmkd	Rotary	541	
10x11	Unwmkd	Rotary		

TYPES OF THE 2¢ WASHINGTON DESIGN OF 1912-20

During the years 1912 through 1920, the 2¢ Washington design pictured below was issued and re-issued with slight variations which gave rise to the many different types of this stamp. Certain of these types, as you will see by comsulting a catalog of United States stamps, are far more valuable than others. The several variations in actual design are pictured and described below. For perforation, watermark and printing variations, see the handy identification chart on the preceding pages.

TYPE I – The ribbon at left above the figure "2" has one shading line in the first curve, while the ribbon at the right has one shading line in the second curve. Button of toga has a faint outline. Top line of toga, from button to front of throat, is very faint. Shading lines of the face, terminating in front of the ear, are not joined. Type I occurs on both flat and rotary press printings.

Type I: Between 406 and 499   Type Ia: 482A, 500   Type II: 454, 487, 491, 539   Type III: 450, 455, 488, 492, 540, 546

TYPE Ia – Similar to Type I except that all of the lines are stronger. Lines of the toga button are heavy. Occurs only on flat press printings.

TYPE II – Ribbons are shaded as in Type I. Toga button and shading lines to the left of it are heavy. The shading lines in front of the ear are joined and end in a strong vertically curved line (arrow). Occurs only on rotary press printings.

TYPE III – Ribbons are shaded with two lines instead of one; otherwise similar to Type II. Occurs on rotary press printings only.

Type IV: 526, 532   Type V: 527, 533   Type Va: 528, 534   Type VI: 528A, 534A

TYPE IV – Top line of toga is broken. Shading lines inside the toga button read "áID". The line of color in the left "2" is very thin and usually broken. Occurs on offset printings only.

TYPE V – Top line of toga is complete. Toga button has five vertical shaded lines. Line of color in the left "2" is very thin and usually broken. Nose shaded as shown in illustration. Occurs on offset printings only.

TYPE Va – Same as Type V except in shading dots of nose. Third row of dots from bottom has four dots instead of six. Also, the overall height of Type Va is 1/3 millimeter less than Type V. Occurs on offset printings only. ·

TYPE VI – Same as Type V except that the line of color in the left "2" is very heavy (arrow). Occurs on offset printings only.

TYPE VII,– Line of color in left "2" is clear and continuous and heavier than in Types V or Va, but not as heavy as in Type VI. There are three rows of vertical dots (instead of two) in the shading of the upper lip, and additional dots have been added to the hair at the top of the head. Occurs on offset printings only.

Type VII:
528B, 534B

TYPES OF THE 3¢ WASHINGTON DESIGN OF 1908-20

Type I: Between 333 and 501

Type II: 484, 494, 502, 541

TYPE I – The top line of the toga is weak, as are the top parts of the shading lines that join the toga line. The fifth shading line from the left (arrow) is partly cut away at the top. Also the line between the lips is thin. Occurs on flat and rotary press printings.

TYPE II – The top line of the toga is strong and the shading lines that join it are heavy and complete. The line between the lips is heavy. Occurs on flat and rotary press printings.

Type III: 529

TYPE III – The top line of the toga is strong, but the fifth shading line from the left (arrow) is missing. The center line of the toga button consists of two short vertical lines with a dot between them. The "P" and "O" of "POSTAGE" are separated by a small line of color. Occurs on offset printings only.

Type IV: 530, 535

TYPE IV – The shading lines of the toga are complete. The center line of the toga button consists of a single unbroken vertical line running through the dot in the center. The "P" and "O" of "POSTAGE" are joined. TYPE IV occurs only in offset printings.

TYPES OF THE 2¢ WASHINGTON DESIGN OF 1922-29

Thin Hair Lines

Type I: Between 554 and 634

Heavy Hair Lines

Type II: 599A, 634A

REGULAR ISSUE OF 1922-32

FRAME		½c thru 15c denominations	17c thru $5.00 denominations
Perf. 11	Flat	551-66 622	567-73 623
	Rotary	594-96	
Perf. 11 x 10		578-79	
Perf. 10		581-91	
Coil 10		597-606 686-87 723	
Perf. 11 x 10½ or 10½ x 11		632-42 653, 684-85 692-96	697-701
Imperf.	Flat	575-77	
	Rotary	631	

GLOSSARY OF TERMS COMMONLY USED
IN IDENTIFYING U.S. STAMPS

BOOKLET PANES are small sheets of stamps sold by the Post Office in booklet form. Most United States postage and airmail panes consist of a block of 6 stamps, or 5 stamps plus a label, that is straight-edged on all four sides but perforated between the stamps as illustrated. Booklet panes are usually collected unused, with the tab, or binding edge, attached.

COIL STAMPS are stamps which come in long rolled strips, especially for use in vending machines, automatic affixing machines, etc. They have straight edges on two opposite sides and and perforated edges on the other two sides. If the straight edges run up and down, the stamps are called "endwise coils"; if they run from side to side, they are called "sidewise coils". Coils are generally collected in singles, pairs or strips of four.

GRILLS are raised impressions made in a stamp by pointed metal rollers, resembling the impressions made in a waffle by a waffle iron. The theory behind the grills used on the United States postage issues of 1867-71 was that the cancelling ink would soak into the broken fibres of the paper, thus preventing the stamp from being washed

clean and used over again. If the frill impression is made from behind, so that the points show on the face of the stamp, the grill is
said to be "points up". If done the opposite way, the grill is said to
be "points down". Grills are further classifide as "Grill A", "Grill
B", etc., according to the type and size of the grill marks on the
stamp. It should be remembered that a complete grill is not always
found on any one stamp. Major varieties with grills are 79-101,
112-122 and 134-144.

Regular Grill   Continuous Marginal Grill   Split Grill

PERFORATIONS around the edges of a stamp are measured by the
number of perforation holes in a space of two centimeters, as "Pert.
11", "Perf. 12", erc. This sounds complicated but actually collectors use a simple measuring device called a perforation gauge which
readily gives this information about any stamp. Where a stamp is
identified by only one perforation number, it is perforated the same
on all four sides; if two numbers are shown (e.g., Perf. 11 x 10½),
the first number indicates the top and bottom; the second the sides.

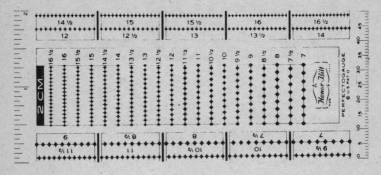

WATERMARKS are faint markings impressed into the paper during
manufacture to help detect counterfeiting. Practically all United
States postage stamps issued between the years 1895-1916 are
watermarked "USPS" (United States Postal Service), either in single
line or double line letters, as illustrated. Before 1895 and since
1916, all postage issues, except for Scott's #519 and some copies of

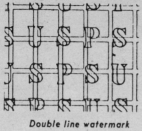 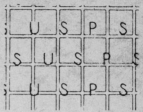

Double line watermark
PERIOD OF USE
Postage 1895-1910

Single line watermark
PERIOD OF USE
Postage 1910-1916

the $1 "Presidential" – an error – are unwatermarked.

To see a watermark, place the stamp on a "watermark detector" and add a few drops of watermark fluid. The watermark – if there is one – will usually show clearly. From the illustrations it can be seen that frequently only a part of a letter will appear.

HOW TO DISTINGUISH BETWEEN FLAT, ROTARY AND OFFSET PRINTINGS.

FLAT PLATE means printed from flat metal plates or engravings.

ROTARY PRESS means printed from plates that are curved to fit around a cylinder. In the curving process, the designs of the stamp stretch slightly in the direction that the plate is curved, so that rotary press stamps issued prior to 1954 are always either slightly wider or slightly taller than the same designs printed from flat plates. Also, on rotary printings, one or more ridges have been forced into the paper to keep it from curling, and these usually show across the back of the stamp. No such ridges are found in flat press stamps.

Left: rotary press issue slightly taller than corresponding flat press design.
Right: rotary press stamp slightly wider than the same design printed from flat plates.

OFFSET is a method of printing in which the plate transfers or "offsets" the design onto a rubber blanket which, in turn, transfers it to the paper. On stamps printed from flat press or rotary press plates (that is, engraved stamps), a relatively large amount of ink is deposited on the paper, giving the stamps a "rough" feeling. If you run a fingernail or metal edge lightly across the lines on such stamps, you can actually feel the ridges of ink. Offset stamps, on the other hand, have a smooth or "soapy" feeling. The ink lies down uniformly on the surface on the surface of the paper, and no ridges can be felt.

SPECIAL PRINTINGS are reprints, either from the original or from new engravings, of stamps previously issued. They are usually printed in limited quantities and for specific purposes, and can almost always be distinguished from the originals by differences in color, perforations, gum, type of paper, etc. The largest single group – the Special Printings of 1875 – consist of a complete set of all designs issued up to that date. They were prepared for display by the government at the Philadelphia Centennial Exposition of 1876. Another good example of a Special Printing is the 1947 "CIPEX" souvenir sheet, shown at the front of this U.S. IDENTIFIER, which was printed as a souvenir of the Centenary International Philatelic Exposition held in New York in May, 1947.

COLLECTOR'S DICTIONARY

Acknowledgment of Receipt Stamp. A stamp used to pay the extra fee that is sometimes required when the sender of a postal item requests a receipt, signed by the addressee, acknowledging the item's safe delivery.

Adhesives. All stamps intended to be affixed to postal matter, as distinguished from postage printed or hand-stamped directly on cards or covers.

Aerogramme. The official Universal Postal Union name for air lettersheets, which are usually carried for less than the normal airmail rates.

Aero-Philately. The collecting of airmail stamps and other airborne mail items; one of the most popular collecting specialties.

Air Cover. See **Flight or Flown Cover**.

Airmail. Postal matter carried by aircraft.

Airmail Stamp. A stamp intended specifically for use on airmail items.

Albino. The uncolored impression of a stamp (usually embossed on an envelope).

Aniline Inks. Extremely bright water-soluble inks derived from coal-tar. Used extensively in stamp printing because they are easily damaged by rubbing and run when wet, thus discouraging attempts to remove cancellations or other markings.

Approval Selections or "Approvals." Stamps sent by dealers to collectors, usually in sheets, books, envelopes, or cards, for free examination. The collector selects the stamps he wishes to purchase and returns the balance to the dealer along with his payment for the stamps he has kept. One of the easiest, quickest, and most popular ways to build a collection.

Arc or Serrated Roulette. A roulette in which the slit is curved in a semi-circle.

129

Arms Types. Stamps bearing coats-of-arms or other heraldic devices; a popular subject among topical collectors.

Arrow Block. A block of stamps containing the arrow-shaped markings used to guide the pane-separator and perforator.

"As is." A term used when selling stamps to indicate that there is no guarantee of condition. Such items should always be carefully inspected before buying, as they are usually non-returnable.

Auction. A public sale at which various lots of stamps are sold to the highest bidder. When the sale is an important one, an **Auction Catalog** describing the various lots is printed and distributed in advance, so collectors at distant points may submit bids by mail.

Backprint. Any printing on the back of a stamp.

Backstamp. A postmark applied to the back of an envelope to indicate the date of arrival at the post office of destination, the location of the post office, and sometimes the exact time or receipt.

Bank Mixture. Mixed stamps, usually still on paper, collected from the incoming mail of banks and other financial institutions. Usually a reliable source of a wide range of foreign stamps.

Bantams. The name given to miniature stamps, especially the war-economy and war-tax issues of South Africa.

Bars. Bars or parallel lines are sometimes used to cancel stamps to indicate that they are invalid, especially in the case of government remainders. They may also be used to obliterate the face value or other details when overprinting.

Bicentennial. A two-hundredth anniversary or its celebration.

Bicolor. A stamp printed in two colors. See **Duty Plate.**

Bilingual. A stamp inscribed in two languages (Canada, Belgium, etc.).

Bilingual Pair. Two joined stamps identical to each other, except that the inscription is in a different language on each stamp (South Africa, South West Africa, etc.).

Bisect. A stamp cut in half vertically, horizontally, or diagonally to be used as two separate stamps, each equal to one-half the value of the whole stamp. Often used in emergencies when stamps of lower denominations are unavailable.

Block. Four or more unseparated stamps forming a square or rectangle; generally understood to consist of four stamps unless otherwise specified, as "block of six," etc.

Bogus Stamps. Imaginary stamps from real or imaginary countries, counterfeited and circulated by swindlers who hope unwary collectors will purchase them as genuine postal issues.

Booklet Pane. A block of stamps, usually six, which originally formed a page in one of the small booklets of stamps sold by the post office.

Border. The outer part or edge of a stamp design.

Bourse. An organized meeting of stamp dealers and/or collectors, at which stamps are sold or traded.

Branding. See **Perforated Initials**.

Broken or Incomplete Set. A group of stamps containing some, but not all of the stamps in a particular issue or series.

"Bulls-Eye" or "Socked-on-the-Nose." A colloquialism used to indicate a stamp with a perfectly-centered and completely legible postmark, usually one with a full town and date cancel.

Bureau Prints or Precancels. Stamps printed or precanceled at the United States Bureau of Engraving and Printing in Washington, D.C., where most U.S. issues have been printed since 1894.

Burelage. A pattern of fine dots or lines on the face (under the design) or back of a stamp to discourage removal of the cancellation or counterfeiting.

Burr. A raised bit of metal on an engraving plate, caused by the engraving tool. If it is not smoothed out or removed, a burr can appear on a sheet of stamps as a printing flaw.

Cachet. A picture, design, or inscription printed or rubber-stamped on an envelope to describe or explain the occasion on which the envelope was mailed, such as the first flight over a new airmail route, first day of issue of a new stamp, the event being commemorated by the new stamp, etc.

Canceled-to-Order or C.T.O. Canceled without having been used for postal purposes. Government remainders are often C.T.O. before sale to dealers, as are many speculative issues.

Cancellation. The ink mark or other defacement (cuts, holes, etc.) on a stamp to show that it has been used once and may not be used again.

Carriers' Stamps. Used in the United States from 1851-63 to pay the delivery fee on postal items from the postal receiving station to the addressee, or from one address to another within the same postal delivery zone, as during those years ordinary stamps only paid the postage from one post office to another.

Catalog Number. The identifying number assigned to each individual stamp of a country by the publisher of a postage stamp catalog.

Catalog Value. The value or "price" assigned to a stamp by the publisher of a postage stamp catalog, usually based on current market conditions.

Centenary or Centennial. A one-hundredth anniversary or its celebration.

Centering. The placement or location of a stamp design with reference to the piece of paper on which it is printed. If the design is squarely in the center, as shown by equal margins of paper on all sides, it is said to be perfectly centered. If one or more margins are much larger than the others, the stamp is said to be **Off-Center**, and is generally regarded as less desirable and valuable than a well-centered copy.

Centimeter or cm. A unit of measurement in the metric system. 2.54 centimeters equal one inch; 100 centimeters equal one meter.

Certified Mail. First class mail for which the sender is given a receipt certifying that the item has been mailed. If desired, a receipt signed by the addressee can also be requested, as proof of safe delivery. There is no compensation for loss of Certified Mail, thus distinguishing it from **Registered Mail.**

Chalky or Coated Paper. A highly-surfaced chalk-coated paper designed to make it impossible to clean off the postmark without removing the stamp design; also used in some humid countries to prevent sheets of stamps from sticking together.

Charity Stamps. See **Semi-Postal Stamps**

"Chop." Japanese characters overprinted, hand-stamped, or handwritten on stamps of territories occupied by Japanese troops during World War II; used until official Japanese occupation stamps became available.

Classic. A stamp, chiefly one issued before 1870, which has gained universal popularity and reputation through widespread philatelic acceptance.

Cleaned. In philately, the term implies that a stamp has had a cancellation or other marking removed for fraudulent re-use or resale as an unused item.

Coarse Perforation. A perforation with large holes and the teeth far apart.

Coil Line Pair. A pair of stamps from a rotary coil showing a colored line caused by a gap where the curved printing plate is joined. Coil Line Pairs are a favorite specialty item. Also called **Joint Line Pair** or **Line-Gap Pair**.

Coil Stamps. Stamps which are issued in long, coiled strips, especially for use in vending or affixing machines. Coil stamps have straight edges on two opposing sides, and perforations on the other two. If the straight edges run up and down, the stamps are called "endwise coils"; if they run from side to side, the stamps are called "sidewise coils."

Collateral Material. Relevant literature and illustrations exhibited with a stamp display to provide additional background information about the stamps in the display.

Color Changeling. A stamp whose color has been altered, either accidentally or intentionally, by chemicals, heat, sunlight, or moisture.

Column. A complete vertical row of stamps from a sheet.

Comb Perforation. A perforation made by a machine which perforates three sides of each stamp in a row at the same time.

Combination Cover. A cover bearing stamps from two countries (Mixed Postage); necessary when mail travels between two non-U.P.U. nations. The first stamp pays postage within the country of origin, the second within the country of destination.

Commemorative Stamp. A stamp issued in remembrance of an event, or as a memorial to some person.

Complete Set. A group of stamps including all the stamps in a particular series or issue.

Compound Perforations. Perforations of two different

measurements on the same stamp. A stamp, for example, which is Perf. 12 on the top and bottom, and Perf. 11 on the sides, is described as Perf. 12 x 11. See **Perforations.**

Condition. The state of being, character, or quality of a stamp, as determined by centering, cancellation marks, cleanliness, etc. The American Philatelic Society recognizes ten degrees of condition: 1. Perfect; 2. Fine; 3. Excellent; 4. Very Good; 5. Good; 6. Average; 7. Fair; 8. Poor; 9. Very Poor; 10. Damaged.

Condominium. A territory ruled by more than one power. Condominium issues may be bilingual, or they may be separate issues of the same design, printed in different languages (Anglo-French New Hebrides, Anglo-Egyptian Sudan, etc.).

Constant. The term used to describe a minor variety which appears in the same place on the sheet throughout multiple printing runs of a stamp.

Control Mark. A letter or numeral placed in the sheet margin, or overprinted on the front or back of a stamp for accounting purposes.

Corner Block. A block of stamps originally located at one of the four corners of a sheet or pane of stamps, and having intact sheet margins on two adjacent sides.

Counterfeit. See **Forgery.**

Counterfoil. Some European stamps, especially parcel post issues (Italy, San Marino, etc.), are printed in two parts, one to be affixed to the item being mailed, and the other, known as a counterfoil, being kept by the sender as a receipt.

Coupon. A postally invalid label or tag attached to a postage stamp, usually carrying a slogan, propaganda matter, or design related to the stamp.

Cover. A complete envelope or card with stamp(s) and cancellation intact.

"Crash" Cover. A cover which has been salvaged from a wreck or crash and delivered to the addressee, usually containing an official inscription explaining the delay.

Crease. A line or mark on a stamp, caused by folding or wrinkling.

Current. The term used to describe stamps which are presently available at the post office.

Cut Cancellation. A cancellation which cuts through the stamp.

Cut Close. A stamp — usually imperforate — with one or

more edges trimmed close to the design, leaving an inadequate margin.

Cut Square or Envelope Cut Square. An embossed or printed envelope, postcard, wrapper, lettercard, or lettersheet stamp cut in a squared shape (allowing ample margin) from the entire piece for the sake of convenience. Cut squares are worth more than the same items cut to their exact shape, but are not worth as much as the entire envelope or piece.

Dead Country. A country which no longer issues stamps, either because it has ceased to exist or because it has changed its name.

Definitives. Stamps used for ordinary postage, and kept in general circulation for a number of years, as distinguished from provisionals, commemoratives, or special purpose stamps. Also called **General** or **Regular Issues.**

Demonetized. A stamp is demonetized when it has been declared no longer postally valid by the issuing authority.

Denomination. The monetary and postal value of a stamp, as "1 cent," "2 shillings," etc.

Departmental Stamps. Official stamps intended for use by one particular government office alone.

Design. The printed portion of a stamp, as distinguished from the surrounding margin of blank paper.

Diamond or Lozenge Roulette. A roulette in which the slits are X-shaped, thus creating a diamond-shaped space between them.

Die. The piece of metal or other material on which the original engraving of a stamp design is made. Multiple reproductions are then taken of the die and put together to form the plate used to print a complete sheet of stamps.

Documentaries. Revenue stamps, formerly used on numerous types of documents (mortgages, wills, bills of lading, etc.) in payment of a government tax.

Double Impression or Double Transfer. The term used when a stamp shows a second impression of the design distinctly overlapping part or all of the first impression.

Dry Printing. A printing method developed in the United States in the 1950's, in which special inks and greater printing pressure allow the use of heavier, stiffer paper with a low moisture content, creating a whiter, high-sheen printing surface which makes the stamp design stand out sharply.

Dues. See **Postage Due Stamps**.

Dumb Cancellation. A postmark which gives neither the date nor the place of cancellation. The term "dumb" is also used to describe stamps which do not outwardly indicate the country or place of origin, and sometimes even the face value.

Duplex Cancellation. A cancellation given in two parts — a cancellation, and a postmark — to ensure the legibility of the date and place name on the postmark.

Duplicate. An additional copy of a stamp. Duplicates should be carefully examined to make sure they are not actually minor varieties.

Duty Plate. One of two plates used in printing bi-colored stamps. The duty plate prints the changing part of the design, usually the value alone, but sometimes other elements as well. The unchanging part of the design is printed by the **Key Plate**.

Electrotype. A method of producing replicas of a die for printing, by applying a coating of copper to a mold taken from the die.

Elusive. The term given to a stamp which is not generally considered to be rare or scarce, but which nonetheless is hard to find.

Embossed Stamps. Stamps in which part or all of the design is raised above the surface of the paper on which they are printed, most commonly used on pre-stamped envelopes.

Engraving. Method of printing using a metal plate into which the stamp design has been cut or etched.

Entire. A stamped envelope, wrapper, postcard, or other postal stationery in its entirety, as sold by the post office.

Envelope Stamp. A stamp printed directly on an envelope, as distinguished from the separately-printed or "adhesive" stamp.

Errors. Stamps with wrong designs, colors, printing, paper, perforations, or over-printing, unwittingly issued by the post office.

Expertize. To make an expert examination of a stamp and render an opinion as to its genuineness.

Express. Special Delivery.

Face Value. The postal value of a stamp as indicated by the figures, words, or abbreviations in the design or surcharge.

Facsimile. An exact imitation or close likeness of a genuine stamp, often created so many collectors can have souvenir or specimen copies of a very rare stamp. Unlike forgeries, facsimiles are openly acknowledged as being only imitations (usually by an inscription on the back), and are not intended to deceive or defraud.

Fake. An originally genuine stamp that has been illegitimately altered by adding or removing perforations, surcharges, overprints, or cancellations, or by changing the color or the value, etc., to increase its philatelic value.

Fine Perforation. A perforation with small holes and the teeth close together.

First Day Cover. An envelope bearing a cancellation date representing the first day of issue of the stamp affixed thereon, and which is usually mailed from the postal station where the stamp was first put into circulation.

First Flight Cover. A cover carried on the inaugural flight over a new airmail route, or an extension of an existing route.

Fiscal. See **Revenue Stamps.**

Flat Plate. A stamp printed on a press with flat plates, as opposed to those printed on a rotary press with curved plates.

Flaw. See **Freak.**

Flight or Flown Cover. An airmail cover.

Forgery. An imitation of a genuine postage stamp, made with intent to deceive or defraud.

Format. The general physical characteristics of a stamp: size, shape, dimensions, etc.

Frame. The outer part or border of a stamp design.

Frank. A mark or label indicating that postage either has been paid, or is free. Most often associated with government or military mail.

Freak. A stamp which shows a production flaw which is not a constant error, such as an ink smudge, a fold or crease in the paper, crooked or off-center perforations, etc. An inconstant minor variety.

Fugitive Inks. Generally aniline inks, used to discourage fakes, forgeries, and fraudulent erasures. They run when wet and become easily damaged by rubbing, so great care is necessary when dealing with such stamps.

General Collector. One who collects all kinds of stamps from different countries, as opposed to a **Specialist.**

General Issue. See **Definitive.**

Granite Paper. A type of safety paper, with tiny colored fibers running through it, to deter forgery.

Grill. A network of embossed or raised impressions made in a stamp by a metal roll with points. The grill is said to be "points up" if the points show on the face of the stamp, and "points down" if they show on the back. Grilling was used on some early United States issues to help the stamp absorb the cancelling inks, thus discouraging fraudulent cleaning.

Groundwork. The background of a stamp design, against which the principal subject is shown.

Guide Dots or Lines. Markings made on the printing plate to guide the pane-separator and perforator.

Gum. The adhesive coating on the backs of most unused adhesive postage stamps.

Gutter. The space between panes on a sheet of stamps.

Handstamped. Stamped or canceled by hand, usually with a rubber stamp but sometimes hand-written, instead of by a machine.

Harrow Perforation. A perforation produced by a machine which perforates the entire sheet of stamps in one operation.

Heliogravure. An early type of photogravure still used in some countries for stamp printing.

Humidor or "Stamplift." A device used to remove stamps from paper without actually immersing them in water. The stamps are placed on a shelf above the water, then covered. The humidity slowly loosens the paper. Preferable to soaking, especially when dealing with old stamps or fugitive inks.

Hyphens. Rectangular-shaped perforations used on some stamps.

Imperforate or "Imperf." Printed without perforations.

Imprint Blocks. A block of stamps with a portion of the sheet margin bearing the printer's inscription, usually his name or initials, but sometimes technical data or other notations.

Inconstant. The term used to describe a minor variety which does not appear in the same place on the sheet through multiple printing runs of a stamp.

Inscription. The letters, characters, or words appearing on a stamp as an integral part of the overall design.

Inscription Block. A block of stamps bearing a marginal inscription relating either to the stamps or to general postal matters, such as "Use Zip Code" or "Mail Early in the Day."

Insured Mail. See **Registered Mail.**

Intaglio. Line-engraving, or recess-printing, so-called because the design is cut into the printing plate and thus is recessed below the surface of the plate. The ink which collects in the recessed design is then transferred to the paper. Line-engraved stamps are easily discernible by feeling with the fingers for the raised ridges caused by the ink making up the design.

Interleaves. Translucent tissue on thin plastic sheets placed between the pages of an album to prevent rubbing. Necessary in albums with stamps mounted on both sides of the pages.

Interrupted or Syncopated Perforations. Used by some countries on stamps intended for use in coil-vending machines. One or more of the hole punches in the perforation machine are removed, leaving a paper "bridge" between the stamps for added strength.

Interverted. The term used to describe a pair of stamps, or a stamp and counterfoil or label, printed or cut in the wrong sequence.

Invalidated. No longer valid for postal use.

Invert. A stamp which has part of the design (usually the central portion) upside down in relation to the rest of the design.

Irregular Perforation. The term used when the perforations on any one side of a stamp are not evenly lined up, or are of different sizes, etc.

Issue. A stamp; also, a related series of stamps, released by a government post office at one time or during a certain period of time.

Journal Stamps. Stamps used to pay bulk postage and sometimes tax on newpapers, magazines, and other periodicals.

Jubilee. A 25th (silver), 50th (golden), or 60th (diamond) anniversary of a ruler's reign or a country's independence, usually the occasion for issuance of a commemorative set.

Key Plate. See **Duty Plate.**

Keytype. A stamp design used in two or more colonies, with only the name and sometimes the value being changed, either by using a different duty plate, or by overprinting. So-called because the common elements of the design are the ones on the key plate.

"Killer" Cancellation. A cancellation which is very heavy and/or covers most of the stamp, effectively disfiguring or obliterating the design.

Label. Coupon . Also used as a disparaging term to describe stamps of dubious philatelic value, as many speculative issues.

Laid Paper. One of the two principal types of paper used for printing stamps. Distinguished by closely parallel horizontal and/or vertical lines created during the paper's manufacture.

Last Day Cancellation. A cancellation made at a discontinued post office on its last day of operation.

Late Fee Stamps. Stamps used to pay the additional postage which is sometimes required when an item is mailed after normal postal hours.

Letterpress. Typography, or relief-printing. The stamp design or a photograph of it **(Photo-Engraving)** is transferred onto a metal plate with a greasy ink; the rest of the plate is etched away, leaving only the raised design. Letterpress-printed stamps can be detected by an impression of the design "standing out" on the back, the result of the raised portions of the plate being pressed into the paper.

Lettersheet. A sheet of writing paper with a stamp already printed on it, so that the sheet can be folded, addressed, and mailed without the necessity for a separate envelope.

Line-Engraving. See Intaglio.

Line Pair. A pair of stamps showing a line of color between them, usually the guide line. See **Coil Line Pair.**

Line Perforation. A perforation made by a machine which only perforates one line at a time.

Line Roulette. The most common type of roulette, consisting of ordinary straight slits.

Lithography. A flat-surface printing method in which the design is drawn, photographed **(Photo-Lithography)** or otherwise transferred to a stone or metal plate, and fixed there via treatment with acid to accept a greasy ink, the rest of the plate being kept damp to reject the ink. Lithographed stamps are distinguishable by their generally flat surface.

Local Stamps. Stamps issued for use only in a certain city, town, or district; not good for postage elsewhere.

Local Precancels. Stamps intended for bulk mailings, precanceled at a local post office to speed mail processing.

Luminescent Stamps. Stamps treated with a phosphorescent substance **(Phosphor Tagged)** or printed on fluorescent paper or with fluorescent ink. Used with electronic machines to speed mail processing.

"Mail Early" Inscription Block. A block of U.S. stamps containing the "Mail Early in the Day" inscription on the sheet margin.

Major Varieties. Stamps differing in one or more major respects — design, color, denomination, shape, size, paper, perforations, watermarks, imprints, inscriptions, etc. — either in the same issue or in different issues.

Manuscript Cancellation. See **Pen Cancellation.**

Margin. The unprinted paper surrounding the design of a stamp; also, the blank paper bordering a sheet of stamps, sometimes called the **Selvedge.**

Marginal. The term used to describe a stamp taken from the extreme top, bottom, left, or right rows of stamps in a sheet, i.e., the rows which directly adjoin the sheet margins.

Master Plate. A printing plate kept as a "master" from which additional printing plates may be made.

Maximum Card. A pictorial postcard showing a stamp design or other subject, bearing either the stamp pictured or a stamp related to the design, and bearing a postmark related to the stamp or subject.

Meter Cancellation. A design printed directly on an envelope or strip of gummed paper (for affixing to mail) by postage meter machine, and used as a substitute for postage stamps. Meter postage is paid in advance, and thus differs from a **Permit**.

Military Stamps. Issued for use by a country's army and military personnel, usually during time of war only.

Millimeter or mm. A unit of measurement in the metric system, equal to one-tenth of a centimeter, and often used in expressing stamp measurements.

Miniature Sheet. A smaller-than-regular-size sheet of stamps; often a **Souvenir Sheet.**

Minor Varieties. Seemingly similar stamps which differ in minor respects such as shade of color or of paper; imperfections in design, printing, or perforations; positioning of watermark or overprint; etc. See **Major Varieties.**

Mint or Mint Condition. A stamp which is in the same physical condition as when it left the mint or printing source or supply: with full, original gum, never hinged, canceled, soiled, stained, creased, marked, or torn.

Mirror Print. An error in which part or all of a stamp is reversed, as in a mirror.

Mission Mixture. Mixed stamps, usually still on paper, collected by mission houses and other charitable organizations. Ususally a reliable source of a wide variety of foreign stamps, and has come to signify any bulk mixture of unsorted stamps.

Mixed Postage. Stamps from two different countries used on the same postal item. See **Combination Cover**.

Mixture. A miscellaneous lot of unsorted stamps, usually containing many duplicates and with the stamps frequently on bits of paper, just as torn from envelopes and wrappers.

Multicolored. A stamp printed in three or more colors.

Multiple. A group of stamps from the same sheet, unseparated, numbering more than two but less than a full sheet.

Multiple Watermarks. A popular form of watermarking, in which a design is repeated so frequently on a sheet that partial watermarks may appear several times on a single stamp.

Mute Cancellation. See **Dumb Cancellation**.

Net. Clear of or free from all deductions.

New Issue. The latest stamp or series of stamps issued currently by a country.

Newspaper Stamps. See **Journal Stamps**.

New Value. An additional value (denomination) added to an existing series; also, a new value surcharged on a stamp of a different original value, creating a "revalued" stamp.

Oblique Roulette. A roulette consisting of parallel diagonal slits.

Obliteration. An overprint used to blot out unwanted parts of a stamp design. See **Bars**.

Obsolete. No longer in use; a term applied to stamps that are no longer being issued or distributed by the post office.

Occupation Stamps. Stamps issued by one country for use in conquered or occupied territory of another country.

Off Center. See **Centering**.

Off Paper. The term used to describe a used stamp which has been removed from the piece of paper to which it was affixed.

Official Seal. See **Post Office Seal**.

Official Stamps. Stamps issued by some countries for use on official government mail.

Offset. A type of lithography in which the design is first transferred from the printing plate to a rubber roller, then from the roller to the paper. See **Lithography.**

Omnibus Issues. A group of stamps, usually sharing a common design, issued by a number of different postal authorities to mark the same occasion. Usually issued by all the colonies of one country, or all the countries in a commonwealth or union (British Commonwealth of Nations, EUROPA, etc.).

On Cover. A stamp still affixed to the entire piece of mail, usually an envelope, on which it was originally used.

On Paper. A stamp still affixed to some of the paper on which it was used.

On Piece. A stamp still affixed to enough of the paper on which it was originally used, to provide philatelic evidence of authenticity, such as a postmark.

Original. A stamp that is not a reprint, forgery, or facsimile.

Original Gum, or O.G. The unimpaired gum with which the stamp was originally issued.

Overprint. Any additional printing (surcharging, hand-stamping, overprinting, etc.) on a stamp after the stamp itself has been printed.

Oxidation. An unintended chemical process by which the original color of a stamp changes, usually through exposure to the elements.

Packet. An envelope or package of stamps, as offered for sale by a dealer. Properly, a packet contains all different stamps, as distinguished from mixtures which usually contain some duplicates.

Packet Cancellation. A special postmark applied to mail carried on a ship maintained or chartered by a government or post office. Differs from a **Ship Cancellation**, which is a postmark applied to mail carried on a private vessel. Both postmarks usually include the name of the ship and/or shipping line.

Pair. Two unseparated stamps; a "vertical pair" when one stamp is above the other, a "horizontal pair" when side by side.

Pane. The so-called "sheets" of stamps sold by post offices are more correctly termed "panes." Most stamps are actually printed in much larger-sized sheets, which are then divided into smaller units, or panes, for distribution at post offices.

Parcel Post. A class of postal service reserved for the sending of packages or parcels, sometimes requiring special **Parcel Post Stamps**.

Part-Perforate. Perforated on two or three sides only. Most coil stamps are perforated on two opposing sides — top and bottom, or left and right; booklet panes stamps are perforated on two or three connecting sides, depending on the location of the stamp in the pane.

Pen Cancellation. A cancellation drawn by hand with a pen or pencil. Also called a **Manuscript Cancellation.**

Perforated Initials or Perfins. Holes punched in a stamp to form letters or a design, used to advertise or to prevent theft. Also called **Branding** or **Punch Perforating.**

Perforations. The holes punched between the rows of stamps in a sheet to facilitate separation. Usually round, but may be square, rectangular, diamond-shaped, etc.

Perforation or Perf. Number. The number of perforated holes in a space of 2 centimeters along the edge of a stamp, determined by using a perforation guage.

Nonprofit
Organization
U.S. Postage
Paid
The American
Film Institute

Permit. A postal system used to facilitate bulk mailings. The sender is licensed to use a registered permit number on his mail in lieu of stamps. He is then charged for the total number of items on which his permit number appears.

Philatelic Agency. A bureau or central point maintained by a government for selling current issues of stamps in quantity to dealers, and in some cases, also to collectors.

Philatelist. A person who collects and studies stamps.

Philately. The technical name for stamp collecting.

Phosphor Tagged. See **Luminescent Stamps.**

Photo-Engraving. See **Letterpress.**

Photogravure. A popular method for printing stamps, in

which a photograph of the stamp design is etched into a metal plate, usually for use on a rotary press (when the process is called **Rotogravure**). Photogravure stamps have the general impression of a photograph, with the design made up of fine dots which can be clearly seen with a magnifier.

Photo-Lithography. See **Lithography**.

Pictorials. Stamps bearing pictures, such as landscapes, animals, flowers, etc., as distinguished from those bearing portraits or symbols.

Pin Roulette. A roulette consisting of tiny pin-holes, with no paper removed.

Plate Number. A file or index number engraved in a plate from which stamps are printed. This number is used to help keep track of the plates, and is usually found in a corner margin of the sheet.

Plate Number Block. A block of stamps with an attached

portion of the sheet margin bearing the plate number. A popular collecting specialty.

Position Blocks. Blocks of four or more stamps which have markings, usually on an attached portion of sheet margin, indicating a position on the sheet, such as plate number blocks, arrow blocks, inscription blocks, etc.

Post Office Seals. Postally-invalid adhesive labels used to re-seal letters or parcels damaged in transit or opened for inspection, or to seal registered items to prevent tampering.

Postage and Revenue. An inscription meaning that the stamps so inscribed can be used for either postage or revenue purposes.

Postage Due Stamps. Special stamps affixed by postal clerks to mail on which the postage was underpaid by the sender. The amount indicated by the stamps is then collected from the addressee upon delivery.

Postal Cancellations. Cancellations showing that a stamp has been used for postal rather than revenue purposes.

Postal-Fiscal. See **Revenue Stamps.**

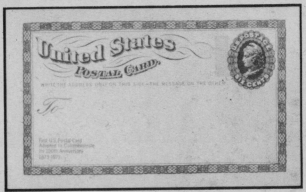

Postal Stationary. Envelopes, postcards, lettersheets, wrappers, lettercards, etc. with stamps officially printed or embossed on them.

HOW TO COLLECT STAMPS

Postally Used. Used for postage, as distinguished from stamps used for non-mail purposes, or cancelled-to-order.

Postmark. A cancellation which usually gives the place and date, and sometimes the exact time of cancellation.

Postmasters' Provisionals. Stamps issued by individual postmasters in various towns and cities, with or without official Post office sanction, and used locally before general postal issues were made available.

Pre-Adhesive. A postal item dating from the period prior to the use of adhesive stamps in a particular country.

Precancels. Stamps cancelled in advance of use, usually with the name of the place where they are to be used, to facilitate the handling of large mailings.

Printed on Both Sides. An error which occurs when a sheet of stamps is accidentally turned over and run through the printing press a second time, so that both sides are "correctly" printed. Not to be confused with **Set-Off**, in which the impression on the back of the stamp is a reverse, or "mirror" image.

Printing. The four most common methods used in printing stamps are: Line-engraving (**Intaglio,** or recess-printing); **Lithography** (usually **Offset** photo-lithography); **Photogravure;** and Typography (**Letterpress,** usually photo-engraving). See separate listings.

Proof. A trial impression taken at various stages of the printing process to make sure that the colors are correct, design is satisfactory, etc., before the actual printing run begins.

Protectorate. A country governed, guided, or protected by a larger, stronger country.

Provisionals or Provisional Issues. Stamps issued or overprinted for temporary use until regular issues are available.

Punch Perforating. See **Perforated Initials.**

Quadrille. Paper containing intersecting vertical and horizontal lines forming small squares or rectangles.

Quartz Lanp. See **Ultraviolet Lamp.**

Railroad Cancellation. A cancellation used on a railway mail car, usually while the mail is in transit.

Recut or Re-Engrave. To remake part or all of a printing plate, to make additions or alterations without materially changing the design.

Redrawn. A redrawn stamp design usually retains all the main characteristics and essential elements of its type, but exhibits minor variations.

Registered Mail. First class mail for which the sender is given a numbered receipt by the post office, ascribing a specific monetary value to the item being mailed (for purposes of compensation in event of loss). A signed receipt is also required of the addressee, certifying safe delivery of the item. **Insured Mail** is similar, but is sent third class.

Registration Stamps. Stamps issued by some countries exclusively for use on registered mail.

Regular Issue. See **Definitives.**

Reissue. A stamp which has been withdrawn from circulation may later be reprinted and reissued by postal authorities.

Remainders. The stamps left on hand in government offices after an issue of stamps has been discontinued. Remainder stocks are usually destroyed, but are sometimes cancelled-to-order and sold to stamp dealers.

Repaired or Mended. Stamps that are damaged (thin spots, creases, tears, etc.) are sometimes very cleverly repaired to hide the damage, usually for fraudulent resale as better-quality items.

Reprint. A stamp printed from the original plates (usually after an issue has become obsolete) but not intended for postal use.

Retouching. Minor repairs made to a printing plate, to mend damaged or worn portions. Usually involves less severe alterations than does recutting.

Revenue Stamps or Fiscals. Stamps affixed to playing cards, tobacco, wines and other spirits, documents, stock certificates, patent medicines, etc., to show that the required government tax on these items has been paid. Revenue stamps used for regular postage are called **Postal-Fiscals**; regular stamps used for revenue purposes are called **Fiscal-Postals**.

Rotary Press. A printing method using curved plates; stamps printed on a rotary press are slightly higher or wider than those printed with flat plates on a flat-bed press, due to the plates stretching slightly when they are being curved.

Rough Perforation. A perforation with jagged holes.

Rouletting. A method of stamp-separation in which slits or pin-holes of various sizes and shapes are made between the rows of stamps without removing any of the paper, thus differing from perforating. See **Arc (Serrated), Diamond (Lozenge), Line, Oblique, Pin, Sawtooth, Serpentine,** and **Zigzag (Point) Roulette** listings.

Safety or Security Paper. Special paper used to make forgery or fraudulent alterations of a stamp more difficult. See **Chalky** and **Granite Papers**.

Sawtooth Roulette. A roulette which leaves angular pointed edges.

Se-tenant. A term applied to two or more unseparated stamps having different values, overprints, or designs, and printed that way intentionally (usually as part of the same set) rather than through an error.

Seals. Postally-invalid adhesive labels usually sold to raise money for various charities. Not to be confused with **Post Office Seals.**

Secret Marks. Microscopic or hidden marks placed in a stamp design by the artist or engraver for identification or reference.

Selvedge. See **Margin.**

Semi-Postal Stamps. Stamps surcharged, overprinted, or inscribed (as above) to obtain funds for various charities, in addition to the usual postal fee.

Separation. See **Perforations** and **Rouletting.**

Series. All the denominations of stamps belonging to a certain issue, as the United States Bicentennial Era Series, often released at different times over a period of months or years.

Serpentine Roulette. A roulette consisting of wavy lines.

Service. When surcharged on a stamp, usually means "on government service," and indicates that the stamp is for use only by a government official.

Sesquicentennial. A 150th anniversary or its celebration.

Set. A number of stamps belonging to a particular issue or series.

Set-Off. A reverse impression on the back of a sheet of stamps, occurring when the sheet has been laid on another sheet whose ink is still wet. Also, reverse impressions transferred to the back of an album page by the stamps on the following page, occurring when the album has been kept for a long time under great pressure. Avoidable through the use of interleaves.

Shade. Slight variations of colors; in philately, taken to mean any variation from the normal color of a stamp.

Sheet of Stamps. The complete sheet as it comes off the printing press. See **Pane.**

Ship Cancellation. See **Packet Cancellation.**

Short Set. A group of stamps from a particular issue or series, usually including all the stamps except for the higher values.

"Sleeper." An unexpectedly elusive or otherwise surprisingly desirable issue.

Soaking. The process of immersing a stamp in water to remove any attached bits of paper; somewhat fallen into disfavor now with the growing use of fugitive inks. If soaking is unavoidable, salt should be added to the water to help retard any running of colors.

"Socked-on-the-Nose." See **"Bulls-Eye."**

Souvenir Sheet. A sheet of one or more stamps specially printed by a government for a specific event or purpose; the margins are usually extra-wide, carrying inscriptions describing the purpose of issue, and the stamps may be perforate or imperforate.

Space Filler. An inferior copy of a stamp, used to fill an album space only until a better copy can be obtained.

Special Delivery Stamps. For use when the sender of a postal item wants it delivered immediately by special messenger, upon its arrival at the post office.

Special Handling Stamps. Stamps for use on fourth class mail, entitling it to the same priority given first class mail.

Specialist. One who collects stamps in a restricted field, such as United States or German stamps only, airmail or revenue stamps only, sports or floral stamps only, etc.

"Specimen" or "Sample." An overprint or perfin applied to postally-invalid samples of a new stamp issue, for distribution to postmasters, philatelic agencies, etc.

Speculative Issues. Many countries today issue stamps less for any legitimate postal use they may see, than for the revenue they will generate through sales to collectors. These stamps are known as speculative issues.

Split. A stamp which has been cut into two or more pieces, each piece to be used as a separate stamp. See **Bisect**.

Split Grille. The term used when a stamp shows parts of two separate grilles.

Spurious. A term used to describe items that are not completely genuine and are used to defraud, such as **Fakes, Forgeries, Bogus Stamps**, etc. **Facsimiles** are generally excluded, as they are not issued for fraudulent purposes.

Stampless Covers. Envelopes, or sheets folded into envelope form with the written message on the inside, which were sent through the mails in the early days before stamps came into use. These covers usually bear postal markings indicating the date the item was mailed and the post office from which it was mailed.

Straight Edge. A stamp with one or two adjacent sides without perforations, caused by cutting the sheet into panes.

"Strike." The impression of a handstamp on an envelope or cover.

Strip. Three or more unseparated stamps in a row, either side by side ("horizontal strip") or one above the other ("vertical strip").

Stuffed Cover. An envelope which has had a card or other stiffening material inserted for protection during cancellation and while in transit.

Subject Collecting. See **Topical Collecting**.

Surcharge. An overprinted revaluation of a stamp, which may include blocking out the original denomination (face value).

Surtax. The added fee on Semi-Postal Stamps.

Syncopated Perforations. See **Interrupted Perforations**.

Tab. See **Coupon**.

Teeth. The projections between perforation holes on a stamp.

Telegraph Stamps. Stamps used to pay telegraph charges or tolls.

Tercentenary. A three-hundredth anniversary or its celebration.

Tete-Beche. The term used to describe a pair of unseparated stamps arranged so that one is printed upside-down in relation to the other. The usual method of printing triangular stamps.

Thematic Collecting. See **Topical Collecting**.

Tied To or On Cover. A stamp affixed to an envelope, card, or wrapper, with a postmark extending over the stamp onto the cover to prove that cover and stamp belong together, and that the stamp was not affixed at another time in a fraudulent attempt to increase its value.

Topical Collecting. The increasingly popular practice of collecting only stamps relating to a single subject or theme, such as Sports, Flowers, Animals, etc.

Torn Stamps. Slightly-torn stamps are generally acceptable as space-fillers, but should otherwise be rejected. In exception are certain issues of Afghanistan, which were cancelled by having the post office clerk tear off a piece of the stamp.

Town or Office Cancellation. The most common type of postmark, giving the name of the post office where (and usually also the date when) the item was mailed.

Typeset Stamps. Stamps printed from regular printer's type,rather than from engraved designs.

Typography. See **Letterpress**.

Ultraviolet, UV, or Quartz Lamp. A lamp producing strong ultraviolet rays, used by experts to check for tampering, aniline inks, or phosphor tags in postage stamps.

Underprints. As an anti-forgery measure, a light color tint or fine repeat design or pattern is sometimes applied underneath the main design of a stamp. See **Burelage**.

Ungummed. Some countries with hot, humid climates issue stamps without gum, as gummed stamps would be too prone to stick together. Other ungummed stamps are normally-gummed issues which have, for one reason or another, lost their adhesive, and usually much of their philatelic desirability as well.

Universal Postal Union or U.P.U. An international opganization formed in 1874, and of which virtually all countries are members. The purpose of the U.P.U. is to regulate international postal matters and facilitate co-operation on such issues as worldwide mail distribution, international postal rates, etc.

Unperforated. Imperforate.

Unused. Not cancelled or otherwise defaced, but not necessarily still in mint condition or with original gum.

Unwatermarked. A term applied to stamps printed on unwatermarked paper.

Used. The term implies a stamp which has been postally-used, as distinguished from cancelled-to-order.

Value. Face Value, when referring to the amount of money for which the stamp was sold at a post office and for which postal service will be rendered; **Market**

or Monetary Value, when referring to its worth as a philatelic commodity.

Varieties. Two or more stamps that are not duplicates. **See Major** and **Minor Varieties.**

Varnish Bars. Lines or bars of clear varnish, sometimes applied to the face of a stamp to make fraudulent removal of cancellation difficult.

Vignette. The main portion of a stamp design, usually the portrait or picture inside the border.

"Wallpaper." A disparaging term used to describe sheets of stamps which have little or no philatelic market value.

Want List. One of the most effective ways for a collector to obtain the stamps he needs is to submit a want list to a dealer, specifying the catalog number, country, value, desired condition, and quantity of each item wanted.

War Tax Stamp. Stamps issued during wartime by some countries, and required to be used on mail in addition to regular postage, the money thus raised being used to help pay the costs of war.

Watermark. A design, characters, letters, numerals, or words impressed into paper during its manufacture, and visible in part or whole on each stamp printed on such paper, though usually only with the aid of a watermark detecting device.

Wove Paper. The most popular used for printing stamps. Distinguishable by its finely netted texture, created during the paper's manufacture.

Wrapper. A sheet of paper, gummed at one end and printed with a stamp, to be used for wrapping and mailing periodicals.

Zig-zag or Point Roulette. A roulette which leaves evenly-shaped pointed teeth along the edges of a stamp.

"Zip Code" Inscription Block. A block of U.S. stamps containing the sheet margin inscription, "Use Zip Code."

FOREIGN NUMERICAL TABLES

CHINESE		ENGLISH
SIMPLE	FORMAL	
半	半	1/2
一	壹	1
二	貳	2
三	叁	3
四	肆	4
五	伍	5
六	陸	6
七	柒	7
八	捌	8
九	玖	9
十	拾	10
百	佰	100
千	仟	1,000
萬	萬	10,000
	分	Cent
	圓	Dollar
貳 佰 圓		$200.
伍 佰 圓		$500.

FOREIGN NUMERICAL TABLES

	ARABIC (ALPHA)	ARABIC (EASTERN)	ARABIC (GOBAR)	ARABIC (HYDERABAD)	ARABIC (TURKEY)	BURMESE
0		٠	٠	٠	٠	
1		١	١	١	١	
2		٢	٢	٢	٢	
3		٣	٣	٣	٣	
4		٤	٤	٤	٤	
5		٥	٥	٥	٥	
6		٦	٦	٦	٦	
7		٧	٧	٧	٧	
8		٨	٨	٨	٨	
9		٩	٩	٩	٩	
10		١٠	١٠	١٠	١٠	
100		١٠٠	١٠٠	١٠٠	١٠٠	

FOREIGN NUMERICAL TABLES

	CYRILLIC (RUSSIAN SLAVONIC)	ETHIOPIAN	HEBREW	INDIAN	KOREAN	KUTCH
0	Г.	◆		0		0
1	Ã.	Õ	א	૧	일	૧
2	В̃.	Ḇ	ב	૨	이	૨
3	Г̃.	Г̲	ג	૩	삼	૩
4	Ã.	Ō	ד	૪	사	૪
5	Ĩ.	Ḝ	ה	૫	오	૫
6	З̃.	Ꝫ	ו	૬	육	૬
7	З̃.	Ẕ	ז	૭	칠	૭
8	Н̃.	Ṯ	ח	૮	팔	૮
9	Ѳ̃	Ṻ	ט	૯	구	૯
10		Ī	י	૧0	십	10
100		Ọ̄	ק	૧૦૦	백	૧૦૦

FOREIGN NUMERICAL TABLES

	MALAY-PERSIAN	MONGOLIAN	NEPALESE	ROMAN	THAI-LAO	TIBETIAN
0	.	০	০		০	০
1	١	᠑	৭ or ৭	I	᠑	༡
2	٢	᠒	২	II	᠒	༢
3	٣	᠒	३	III	᠒	༣
4	٤	᠔	৪	IV	᠔	༤
5	৫	᠕	৭ or ৭	V	᠕	༥
6	٦ or ৬	᠖	৬ or ৬	VI	᠖	༦
7	٧	᠗	৩ or ৩	VII	᠗	༧
8	٨	᠘	৮ or ৮	VIII	᠘	༨
9	٩	᠙	৯ or ৯	IX	᠙	༩
10	١.	᠑᠐	৭০	X	᠑᠐᠗	༡༠
100	١..	᠑᠐᠐	৭০০	C	᠑᠐᠐	༧༠༠

168

Key Map

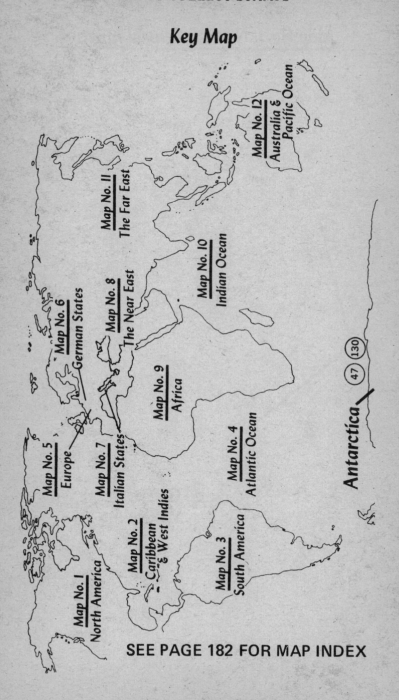

Map No. 12
Australia &
Pacific Ocean

Map No. 11
The Far East

Map No. 10
Indian Ocean

Map No. 6
German States

Map No. 8
The Near East

Map No. 9
Africa

Map No. 5
Europe

Map No. 7
Italian States

Map No. 4
Atlantic Ocean

Map No. 2
Caribbean
& West Indies

Map No. 1
North America

Map No. 3
South America

Antarctica (47) (130)

SEE PAGE 182 FOR MAP INDEX

Map No. 1: North & Central America

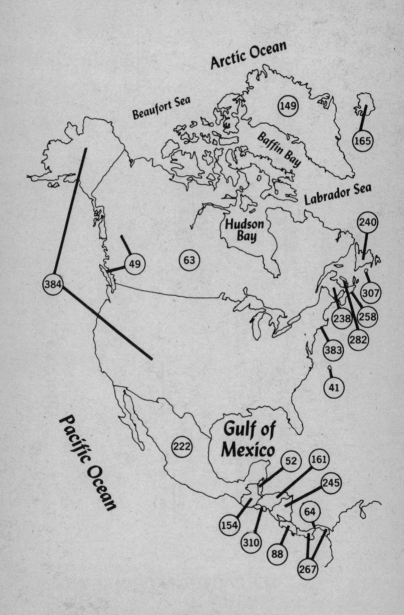

Arctic Ocean

Beaufort Sea

149

165

Baffin Bay

Labrador Sea

Hudson Bay

240

49

63

307

384

238 258

282

383

41

Gulf of Mexico

222

52 161

245

64

154

310 88

267

Pacific Ocean

Map No. 2: Caribbean Sea & West Indies

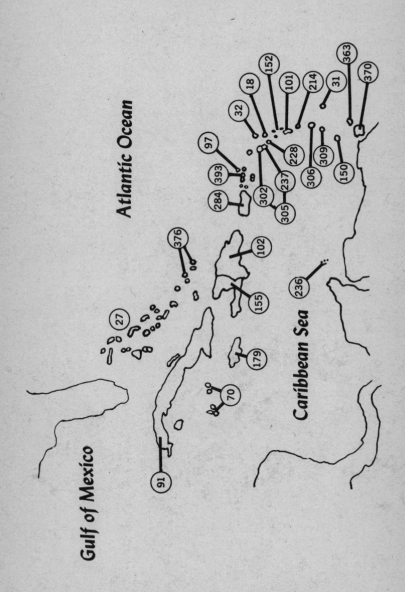

Map No. 3: South America

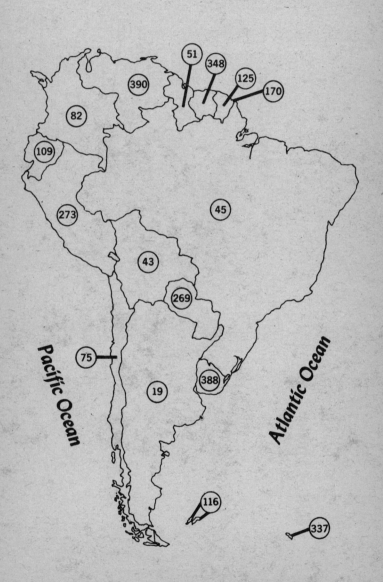

Map No. 4: Atlantic Ocean

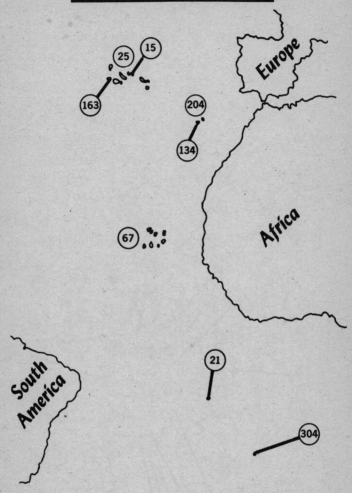

Map No. 5: Europe

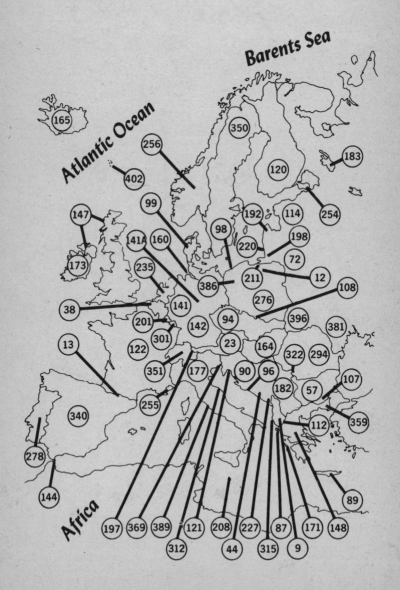

Map 6: German States

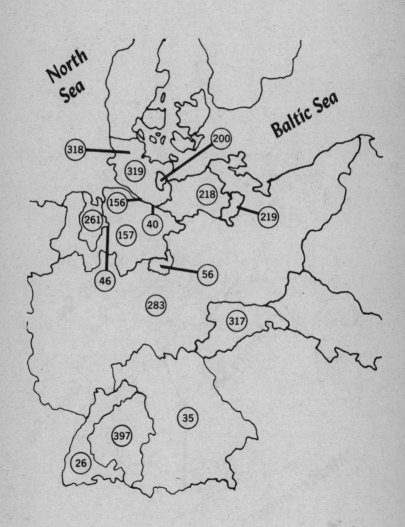

North Sea

Baltic Sea

318
319
200
156
261
218
219
157
40
46
56
283
317
35
397
26

(detail of Map No. 5)

Map 7: Italian States

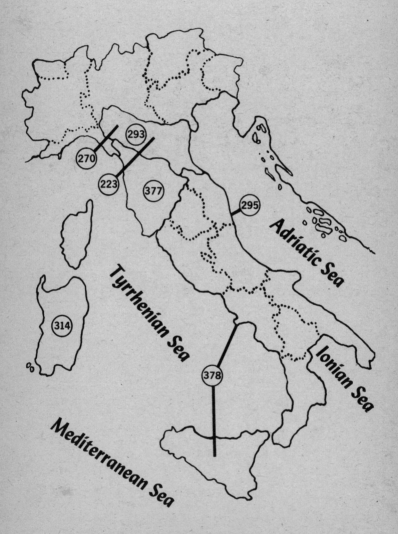

(detail of Map No. 5)

Map 8: The Near East

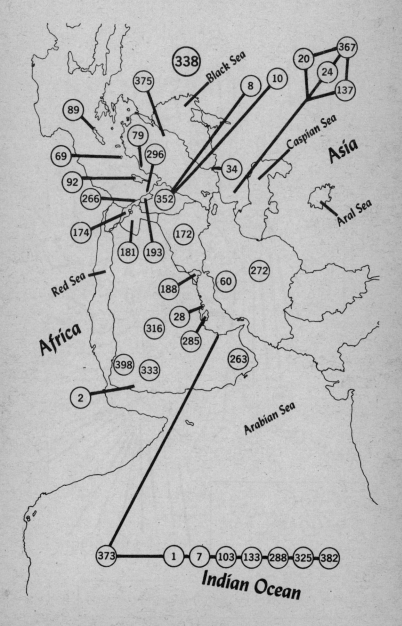

Map 9: Africa

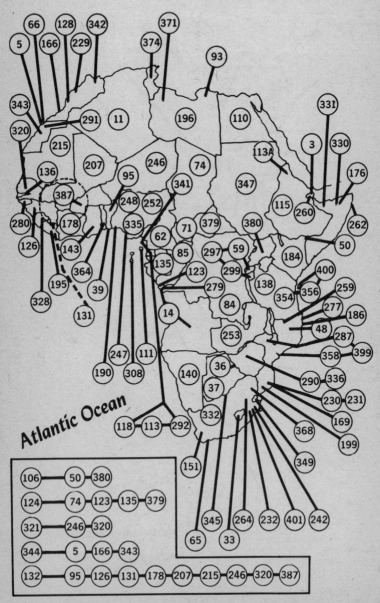

Map No. 10: West Indian Ocean & Arabian Sea

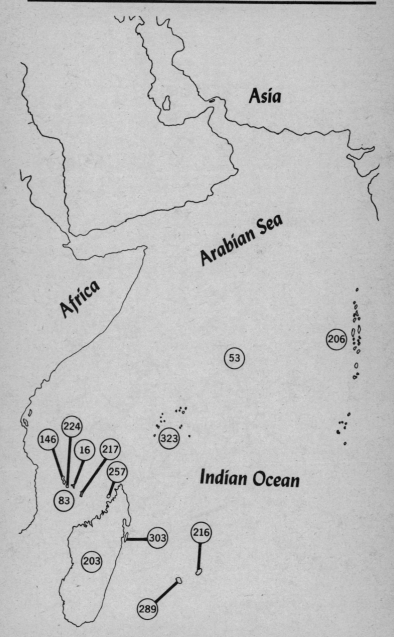

Asia

Arabian Sea

Africa

206

53

224

146

16   217

257

323

Indian Ocean

83

303   216

203

289

Map No. II: The Far East

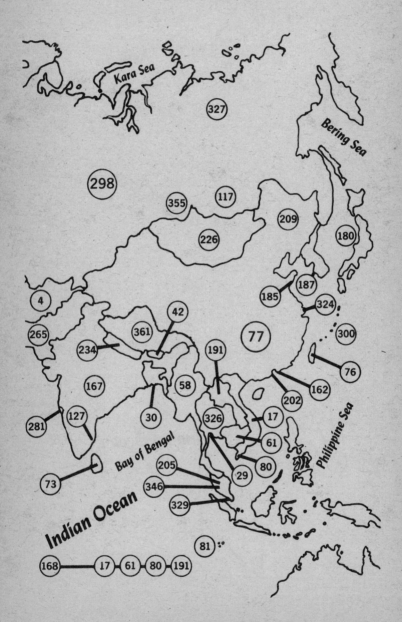

Map No. 12: Australia & South Pacific Ocean

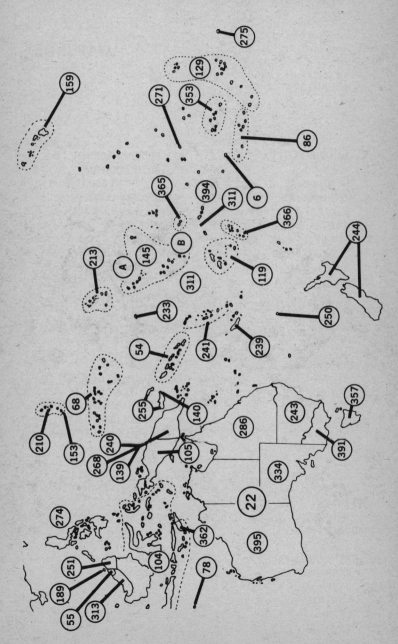

MAP INDEX

HOW TO COLLECT STAMPS

HOW TO COLLECT STAMPS

84

NOTES

NOTES

NOTES